The Church of the Third Millennium

The Church of the Third Millennium

A Straight-talking Guide to the Postmodern World and its Impact on the Church

Philip Hill

paternoster
press

First published in 1999 by Paternoster Press

Reprinted in 2000

05 04 03 02 01 00   7 6 5 4 3 2

Paternoster Press is an imprint of Paternoster Publishing,
PO Box 300, Carlisle, Cumbria, CA 3 0QS, UK
http:www.paternoster-publishing.-com

British Library Cataloguing in Publication Data
A catalogue record for this book is available from the British Library

ISBN 0–85364–948–0

Cover Design by Mainstream, Lancaster
Typeset by Westkey Ltd, Falmouth, Cornwall
Printed in Great Britain by
Caledonian International Book Manufacturing Ltd, Glasgow

To Rachel, Matthew,
Jonathan and Abigail
whose Christian lives will be lived in
the third millennium.

Contents

Part One

The World We Live In

One

A Crisis for Evangelicals

The third millennium is almost upon us. Some Christians believe it will be the millennium of Revelation 20, verses 1–6, expecting Jesus to return and reign for a thousand years on earth. There are in fact other ways to understand the 'millennial reign' of Christ, but however much Christians may differ about the issue, one thing is certain: Jesus said of his visible return *'No one knows about that day or hour, not even the angels in heaven, nor the Son, but only the Father'* (Mt. 24:36).

Perhaps it will be soon. I hope so. But even if we are convinced it is on the next horizon we must be prepared to wait longer and face the challenge of another generation – or even another millennium – of Christian life and witness. Martin Luther, the founder of German evangelical Christianity in the sixteenth century, put it wonderfully. He once said that even if he expected the Lord to return tomorrow he would still plant an acorn today. That is the purpose of this book. It is to plant the acorn of a new vision for evangelical life and witness for the new millennium.

Why is a new vision necessary? There are two reasons. One concerns a fundamental change in Western life generally, the other concerns the current state of evangelical life.

The Change in Western Life

We are living through a revolution. It is not a political upheaval but rather a massive change in the beliefs on which people base their understanding of life. Academics call this revolution 'post-modernism', but it is not an academic movement so much as a new mood and style which affects every one of us.

For centuries, Christians of all traditions have been able to assume the Western world 'talks the same language' as the church. We still disagree over some very fundamental issues but we all share the benefits derived from nearly two thousand years of Christian influence. That is what has now changed. Sure enough, people are still using the same words; the trouble is they are giving them different meanings. Two examples will help to illustrate the problem.

Take the word 'spiritual'. For over a thousand years it has meant something like 'unusually close to God'. In the last ten years it has come to mean 'sensitive to the non-rational'. Morality, belief, even consistency do not matter. What does matter is being in touch with the mysterious. That is why so many famous and influential people affirm 'spirituality' by visiting psychics and astrologists and at the same time reject personal morality.

Another term which has changed its meaning is 'I feel'. Traditionally, human expression has been regarded as having three dimensions: mind, will and emotion. The mind was regarded as superior and led the way in knowing truth. The will followed as choices in life were based on understanding. The emotions were last, on the understanding that we felt things whether they were true or not, important or not, chosen or not.

In the postmodern world, feeling and understanding have changed places. Something is true if it feels right. If it feels right, we should believe and act on it (for today at least) – choices – the will – follow emotion. The least dependable thing is understanding. Ideas are now seen as changeable and uncertain, liable to lead us away from the 'real world' of personal experience. Understanding has thus replaced emotion as the realm of personal expression – it produces not just subjective but unreal 'ideas'. And emotion has taken the place of understanding as the realm of what is real – it is an experience rather than 'just an idea'.

The Current State of Evangelicalism

The traditional view of human self-expression is firmly entrenched in evangelical theology and has strong biblical credentials. That has led some conservative evangelicals to close their minds to the fundamental shift which is taking place in society in order to reject anything which smacks of compromise with modern unbelief. In fact, that approach confuses two distinct issues.

The first is spiritual unbelief, which the apostle Paul analysed as ultimately caused because '*the god of this age has blinded the minds of unbelievers, so that they cannot see the light of the gospel of the glory of Christ*' (2 Cor. 4:4). His answer – and it must be so for every biblical Christian – was the supernatural power of God, who '*made his light shine in our hearts to give us the light of the knowledge of the glory of God in the face of Christ*' (2 Cor. 4:6).

The second issue is cultural relevance. The gospel always has been preached to different cultures in ways those cultures can relate to. The unchanging message of the gospel has to be addressed to a changing world in ways the world can understand. That has demanded times of change within the Christian Church. As Greek was replaced by Latin in the Roman world the Bible was retranslated and worship was adapted to use familiar music and language. Many centuries later Latin language and music became unfamiliar and they were replaced by hymns in common speech, and more recently those too have been marginalized or at least added to by modern songs.

I recently heard a Bible translator illustrate how great the task can be to communicate the biblical message in a different culture. He was translating the New Testament for a tribe which had never seen sheep. When he came to 'behold the lamb of God' he had to choose between inventing a word for sheep and then leaving readers with no mental picture of a lamb, or using a word for an animal they were familiar with whose young were white and innocent-looking. Was he making the Bible clearer or not? That is the challenge of cultural adaptation. Although the Holy Spirit reveals the truth to the mind of unbelievers, he uses the relevant proclamation of the gospel in doing so. Relevance and faithfulness to Scripture are not alternatives but partners in the work of mission.

Evangelicalism is in trouble on both counts. It has become so diverse a movement that it is difficult to agree what the core beliefs which demand faithfulness are. It has also become trapped in its own cultural world, which once was highly effective and relevant to the wider world but now is increasingly distant. Evangelicalism is, of course, a world movement. However, it is originally an English-speaking one and my focus will be on the British scene. I fully recognize that people from other cultures may have different stories to tell, though the links are still strong at an international level because of our enormous missionary activities.

Liberal trends

With regard to belief, evangelicalism has developed its own brand of liberal Christianity. It rejects the bold statement that the Bible is not true, but increasingly empties it of doctrine. It rejects the distortion of Jesus as only a good man, but substitutes it with one of God as only a nice God. It rejects the idea of abandoning biblical morality but calls it an ideal rather than a rule. It despises dependence on the latest scholarship but will believe virtually anything said by the latest evangelical or charismatic superstar. Worst of all, it has reduced conversion from loving Christ to liking him, from a life of service to him to a life of service from him. All the suffering and dying must be done by Jesus. The Christian is asked to receive only blessing and happiness.

The result of this trend is an evangelical movement increasingly wary of distinctives, lacking in passion and shy of sacrificial service. Success is too often equated with popular appeal, failure with rejection by the world. It is bland, ineffective and ultimately boring. Churches which succumb to it have to pack their programmes with more and more entertainment and trivial pursuits in place of living for the kingdom of God. Instead of becoming like little children to enter the kingdom of heaven, we are invited to enter the kingdom of heaven and spend the rest of our lives behaving like little children who must never be taught, corrected or have demands which invade our personal freedom made upon us. This will not challenge the next generation to turn to Christ, for it does not even portray Christ honestly.

While evangelicals frequently pour scorn on ecumenism based on the 'lowest common denominator', we have begun to develop something very like it. Bible-believing Christians hold different convictions about some very important matters which shape the whole of our Christian lives. They include baptism, church order, the second coming and the relationship between Christianity and society. As a result, these subjects are becoming controversial or even 'no-go areas' in preaching and teaching. I have been accused of divisiveness, for example, when preaching believer's baptism in a Baptist church because so many members come form paedo-baptist backgrounds.

It would not matter so much if Christians could still find definite ways of living out their faith and churches were able to continue in stability. But they can't. Churches need a clear identity in order for people to remain united within them. Furthermore, Christians need to choose some definite understanding of life in the world, otherwise they will choose no Christian understanding at all. In this vacuum the new distinctives are increasingly pragmatic and feeling based. People often join the church which 'feels right for them' and even follow leaders rather than principles.

This is especially true of charismatic life. Indeed, some would say it is God's provision to communicate the faith in a postmodern society based on experience rather than ideas. The trouble is that doctrinal belief easily becomes regarded as unimportant and even divisive, unlike the New Testament itself which tests experience by doctrine and not the other way round. And while it is true that charismatic life relates well to the current preference for experience over 'dogma', it might be said to relate too well. Does it challenge postmodernism or give in to it?

Some evangelicals recognize these trends but fall instead into the traditionalist trap. While a few are turning in frustration to the Catholic or Orthodox traditions, we have our own tradition-alist movement – the Elizabethan Bible, the eighteenth-century hymnbook and the nineteenth-century order of service. It drives evangelicals into a faithful but irrelevant corner of society where few are saved because few non-Christians can understand what is being done or said.

Shaped by its roots

That brings us to the second great problem with evangelicalism today. The term 'evangelical' has become so closely associated with 'Bible-believing' that we often think they are interchangeable. That is not really true, however. The evangelical movement as we know it began only in the eighteenth century. Before that, the claim to represent 'biblical Christianity' was made by church bodies rather than by an informal and interdenominational movement. Modern evangelical life is still profoundly shaped by those roots.

Firstly, they have caused evangelicalism to remain primarily a movement for evangelism and discipling. It began as a force for renewal within the Anglican Church and spread among Christians from other denominations as well. Consequently, it has never developed distinctive teachings about church related issues such as ministry, the sacraments and church order. Churches sometimes adopt the word 'evangelical' as a description of themselves, but in fact the description is always inadequate because other distinctives remain necessary regarding such things as baptism and church order. Nor have we been united about non-conversion issues like the sovereignty of God, the second coming or the baptism of the Spirit. Yet these matters are of fundamental importance within the New Testament and are a practical necessity both for church unity and for living the Christian life with integrity.

Some evangelicals have even made their particular views a test of genuine belief in the Bible. This has notably been the case with more fundamentalist groups. I was converted through a 'free evangelical' church which insisted that every member equated belief in the second coming with premillennialism. Down the road was an equally fundamentalist and premillennialist Pentecostal fellowship. Further down the road was a free evangelical but Calvinistic church. As good premillennialists we were encouraged to revere non-Christian Israel more than those other churches! The same disrespect for other evangelicals has been more than occasional in charismatic life.

Secondly, the history of evangelical life has encouraged solidarity through non-denominational rather than denominational involvement. Evangelicals tend to gain identity and inspiration from para-church organizations and from national events like Keswick, Spring Harvest and March for Jesus. In doing so, we have sometimes tended towards creating a subculture which stands apart not only from the world at large but from the mainstream churches as well. At times, evangelicals have developed quite strict extra-biblical rules for personal conduct – though these are going out of fashion as the 'cost of discipleship' theme is replaced by 'the benefits of believing'.

The ease with which evangelicals pour money and time into new movements does not always strengthen solidarity, however. It has fragmented evangelical life as much as unified it. We have a sorry record of allowing gifted leaders to build agencies where their influence is unchecked. Whole denominations and missionary bodies have arisen to represent either a peculiar emphasis or even the exclusive authority of an individual leader.

Most significantly of all in the postmodern age, is a third result of our beginnings. Evangelicalism is the product of not only its internal history but also the world of thought in which it began. The eighteenth century saw the birth of the modern world, which focused especially on the rights of the individual and the pursuit of scientific learning and 'rational thought'. Evangelicalism has challenged this way of understanding very effectively but it has bought into it as well.

When, for example, humanists declared 'man' to be the highest form of life, evangelicals replied with the biblical accusation of our human sinfulness and accountability to God. Yet evangelicals also accepted the humanist idea in several ways. They affirmed it by stressing in a new way that conversion was above all a personal experience of God's personal love. Previous generations would have made more of conversion into the church, retaining the central place it is given in the New Testament.

The same weakness occurred with regard to the pursuit of scientific and rational thought. Evangelicals have challenged the ultimate authority of human intellect by teaching the moral and intellectual blindness of people without God. At the same time, there was a strong reaction against the accusation that evangelicals were 'enthusiasts', an old English word for 'emotionalist'. Where older generations retained respect for the miraculous and for mystical experiences of God, the evangelical movement became more wary, even rejecting them as impossible. This fitted the age of reason, but only because it came from the age of reason rather than the Bible.

The challenge of postmodernism

Postmodernism presents a fundamental challenge to evangelical life. It questions the value of understanding and so undercuts the proclamation of doctrine. It dismisses the importance of rational truth and so leaves evangelicalism isolated by its insistence on intellectual clarity. Evangelicals are still more preoccupied with personal piety than life in the church; with rational belief than receptiveness to the supernatural; with disciplined living than responsiveness to a divine impulse.

Of course, it is not only evangelical Christianity which is at risk. The postmodern world is neither capable of distinguishing between evangelicals and others, nor very much interested in doing so. It is worth setting ourselves in the broader context of Christian tradition and its relations with the modern world, in order to see how we have been influenced by that as well.

At the beginning of the twentieth century Christianity seemed triumphant. It had experienced a century of expansion both at home and abroad. It dominated public life to the extent that it was followed by great leaders and had spread to every continent. After two world wars, with the Great Depression between them, people stopped going to church. After the youth revolution of the sixties, children stopped going to Sunday School.

Since then, we have witnessed even more radical changes. With the growth of a multi-cultural society the Bible is no longer taught in schools. With the collapse of traditional morality people no longer agree what is right or wrong. In a world with competing ideologies, contrasting cultures and incompatible religions, no one is allowed to say there is absolute truth at all, least of all the Christian Church which is itself perceived as hopelessly divided and confused. To the unbeliever, we Christians now seem ridiculously enslaved to the past. They regard our services as irrelevant, our buildings as museums, our morality as outdated and our claim to be right as arrogant.

In part, they are correct. Christianity is all too often locked into the past. Too many churches keep exclusively to past forms of language and music. But there have already been several attempts to come to terms with the decline of Christianity in the Western world. The trouble is they have not been particularly successful either in halting decline or in clarifying the gospel to the world at large.

The first response came in the form of 'liberalism'. This movement recognized how the world was changing as long ago as the early nineteenth century and sought to present the gospel in ways the 'modern world' could understand. It gave more to Christianity than evangelicals are prepared sometimes to admit. But it has gone too far in reducing the Bible to purely human authority and presenting Jesus as only one of several great religious teachers, undermining and sometimes even denying the seriousness of rejecting him as Saviour and Lord. The aim was to communicate the gospel to the world but it often sounded more like an admission that the gospel was wrong in the first place. That is certainly what many non-Christians have concluded from liberal Christianity.

Another response to the loss of respect for Christianity is the ecumenical movement. Its inspiration is Jesus' prayer that his disciples may be one so that the world may believe. The reality is that the world has not believed any more than before. The media has not even noticed the ecumenical movement except when it has blundered, like a recent international assembly which was reported internationally because pagan religious rites were used in worship. Critics have some justification for observing that this is not calling the world to believe in Christ but to not having to believe in him at all.

Not all Christians have accepted these trends. The third main strand in modern Christianity is a renewed interest in ancient Christian tradition. As society drifts away from the church, a number have responded by rejecting modernity altogether. Some have adopted Catholic worship while remaining Protestants, especially in the Anglican Church. Others have moved into Catholic Church life completely. In Britain, interest has grown in what is presented as ancient 'Celtic Christianity'. Still others have turned to the Othodox Churches of Russia and Greece. Several prominent evangelicals have done this, including Michael Harper in Britain and Franky Schaeffer in America. It is a beguiling world increasingly attractive to those who seek a visible expression of spiritual mysteries and who are rightly critical of the shallow popularism so common in evangelical church life now.

The need for change

This is a book about evangelical belief and church life in the Western world. I am well aware that there are other Christian traditions and magnificent stories of church life elsewhere in the world, but my concern is to address my own people and their future. I do so in the conviction that evangelicalism is in need of change rather than destruction.

The Christian faith is shaped by three main factors: Scripture, the long history of Christian tradition and contemporary response to them both. All Christians have to make judgements about the balance between them. Catholic and Orthodox life give first place to Christian tradition, while the historic Protestant churches have increasingly placed contemporary relevance higher than biblical orthodoxy. Evangelicals have maintained the priority of Scripture over both contemporary thought and tradition. I am committed to that position as the only one which faithfully represents the authority and the message of Jesus Christ.

The purpose of this book is to ask what kind of church we need to be if we are to fulfil this task for the next generation. How are we to 'go into the world' of postmodernism without being lost in it? How are we to disciple people who regard discipline as an intrusion of freedom? How are we to teach everything Jesus commanded to people who reject understanding in favour of feelings? How are we to be the authentic church of Jesus Christ in the third millennium?

Two

Living in the World of Nothing-Buttery

Our Confusing World Today

I started my ministry in 1971 in a Welsh country village. Only around a hundred people came to services out of a population of some three thousand. But everyone knew the minister and welcomed pastoral support in times of need. My biggest congregations were at funerals, when it was common for three hundred to pack the old Baptist chapel. The singing was strong because people knew the usual hymns from childhood attendance at Sunday school. Religion meant Christianity. I could go into a Religious Education class at the local school knowing that every child knew about Jesus and the Bible in some basic way at least.

These days I conduct all too many funerals where even the most popular hymns cannot be sung by the few people who turn up. When I visit local schools, I am asked to explain things like when Jesus lived and what Christians do in church, taking my turn among representatives from other world religions, including sometimes a local witch.

On one recent occasion a girl of fourteen listened intently through a discussion about why God allows evil. When I invited questions her response to this profound issue was to ask with the utmost sincerity, 'Why are you wasting your life being a minister when religion is nothing more than personal opinion anyway?' The teacher who had invited me turned a rather bright shade of purple, but I was more intrigued than offended. I asked her why she thought like that about religion. 'Well, sir', she replied, 'everything is, isn't it?'

My questioner had as little confidence in science as religion, as little regard for the institution of the family as the church, as despairing a view of life without God as life with him. Everything came down to 'do it if you like', but not if you don't. The whole of reality was reduced in her mind to how it felt for her. I could tell from the reaction among the others that her view was widely shared.

Nor is this new mood in society limited to people who do not study or think deeply. I recently heard about a university student who explained how he approached his degree studies. He said, 'I never accept anything as true unless it feels right.' This is the world we now live in. There are no truths worth serving and no causes worth following on principle. The meaning of life is in feeling good about something because everything in life has been reduced to nothing but a personal opinion. It is the world of 'nothing-buttery'.

Only a generation ago the great obstacle to Christianity in the Western world was faith in science and confidence in human ability. People who could read about the origins of the world in a science textbook rejected God as Creator. People who believed in themselves and the 'inevitable progress' of the human race did not see the need for salvation. That was the generation which thought that the meaning of life was certain and that it did not include God.

No such certainty exists any more. There is no more promise of life before death than life after death. The challenge to Christianity today is not that there is something more certain, but that there is nothing certain at all. When Christians say that Jesus Christ is the truth it is no longer the meaning of 'Jesus Christ' which most confuses people but the meaning of the word 'truth'.

In such a world as this, the best you can manage is to do whatever makes you feel good about yourself today. That is why the centre of community life is now the shopping mall. Shopping makes people feel good about themselves – not the security of owning things but the momentary pleasure of buying them. The

mall has replaced the church as the place to go to experience
meaning and purpose in life. Perhaps that is why shoplifting has
escalated so much. If you can't get you don't belong and you can't
enjoy life. The immoral thing to such people is not stealing but
being excluded from the central activity of life.

You see the same trend away from truth in favour of feelings
in politics. At one time the different parties held fundamental
beliefs which they sought to work out in public life. During the
eighties they began to aim more at producing a 'feel-good factor'
than at working out principles. There are no great principles of
any kind except that of keeping the electorate feeling good. The
public mood is everything, because there are no moral foundations left by which society is willing to be governed. We are
confronted here as everywhere else with 'nothing-buttery'. Truth,
morality, virtue – all of them are nothing but what one person
chooses to believe while someone else, equally reasonably,
chooses not to believe. Our society is dying of a moral cancer
caused by its loss of faith in everything.

The influence of existentialism

The rejection of religion in favour of secular values began early
in this century. On its own it would not have produced the
postmodern world where science and technology have become as
suspect as religion. That change was brought about through the
philosophy known as existentialism, of which two French writers,
John Paul Sartre and Albert Camus were major representatives.
You may never have read their books or even heard of existentialism, but you know the ideas they and others expressed. They
taught us to live for the moment, despise rules, suspect authority,
question every claim to 'truth' and assert the value of individual
freedom over every other value in life.

At its best existentialism was idealistic and compassionate. At
its worst it was a fine excuse for doing whatever one liked no
matter what the consequences. An outstanding existentialist film
of the sixties was *The Graduate*. The music for the film was
provided by the existentialist singer-songwriters Simon and

Garfunkel. The star was Dustin Hoffman, another existentialist cult figure. He portrayed a brilliant law student who graduated with the highest honours and returned home to join his father's law firm.

He was soon dissatisfied with his privileged lot in life and dismayed by the hypocrisy of his parents and the pointlessness of suburban American life. He fell into an affair with Mrs Robinson, the wife of his father's partner. He then fell in love with her daughter. The final scene takes place at her wedding to 'the right type of man' who is a dull, colourless and unfeeling bore. Hoffman invades the service and drags away his love, grabbing a large cross to fend off the infuriated family and guests. Having shown contempt for religion, family values, normal life and stability, the film closes with the couple making their escape on a passing bus, the ultimate symbol of having no money or possessions. That is existentialism.

In the eighties, idealistic existentialism was well and truly rejected by the very people who followed it in their youth. If *The Graduate* portrayed the youth of the sixties in rebellion, the cult TV series *LA Law* portrayed the same kind of people twenty years later and approaching middle age. It is as if 'the graduate' lawyer finally wised up and sold out to materialism. It is certainly what happened to that generation. For all their rejection of religion and morality, they repented of idealism in favour of success at all costs. The eighties were the years of total cynicism and selfishness, when people who got hurt in the process went to a counsellor to find out how to become more self-assertive than ever.

The return of religion

Surprisingly, however, the mood has changed in the last decade of the century. Sociologists confidently used to predict the complete demise of religion, especially among the professional middle classes. They based their assumption on the idea that education would show belief in God to be unnecessary and prosperity would make it irrelevant. In fact, religion in the West has grown in popularity most among those very people. It has been a major upset in sociological predictions and experts are still seeking ways to explain it. Christianity could save them a great deal of trouble! There is no such thing as an irreligious society because God has created humanity with an inborn longing for spiritual reality.

The crucial factor now, however, is that religion has returned and not just Christianity. That tells us something about the postmodern view of reality. Nothing can be known with certainty and therefore religious certainty is viewed with suspicion. But that does not mean religion is not real. After all, religion is also about experience and experience is real. So religion is 'OK' as long as you don't get dogmatic about it and tell other people yours is the only one which is right. On the other hand you can tell them that yours works for you and maybe it will work for them as well. We are back to the cynical idea that nothing can be known with certainty – like the fourteen-year-old schoolgirl I encountered. It is a devastating approach to life because it undermines the simplest and most basic aspects of living.

The world of 'nothing-buttery' is one where every claim to the truth is reduced to 'nothing but an idea' and a personal opinion at that. There are no certainties except the certainty of personal experience. We can never know whether our personal experience is right so we have to be content to say that it is right for us – maybe not for anyone else.

An opportunity for evangelism?

From one point of view, the postmodern world provides a great opportunity for Christian witness. Because so much attention is now paid to finding meaningful experience in life, Christianity has a ready point of contact with people through teaching the true experience of God. This is part of the explanation for the growth in charismatic church life and especially the staggering success of Alpha courses. It is no accident that these movements are appealing to middle class and educated people. They are the ones who are most conscious that the spiritual vacuum in modern society is not filled either by material success or advanced education.

However, there are dangers in playing to the gallery. If we speak of experiencing God and Christ we connect with our society provided we accept that it is only one way of finding spiritual reality. If we assert the finality of Scripture and the Lordship of Christ we run counter to it. Other religions may genuinely be able to take their place alongside each other as alternative ways to experience God, but Christianity claims something much more. It is because Jesus is Lord that Christianity is true and it because Christianity is true that it leads to a genuine experience of God. Nor is it simply a matter of Christianity being true. The truth concerns the death of Christ for sinners. The experience of God is that of forgiveness for sin and new birth in Christ. Before that comes another experience – repentance from both our sins and our futile attempts to please God by ourselves.

The gospel is first a message of condemnation before it is a promise of love and acceptance. Without the awful declaration that human nature is sinful and separated from God, the gospel is no more than a version of modern counselling: a way to cope with life's problems more effectively. Do you want to feel good about yourself? Come to Jesus because he loves you. Do you want to solve your marriage problems? Turn to God and he will help you. Do you want to be healthy and happy? Jesus heals and blesses those who come to him.

This is the gospel too often preached by evangelicals today. It undoubtedly leads to feelings of well-being, peace and greater happiness in life. But that is the problem. The postmodern world loves experience and will easily respond to such wonderful promises. The New Testament message, however, is a different one. Salvation does not merely help us to live, it changes us and turns us from the pursuit of self – even the happy self – to the pursuit of God. Many 'converts' do not survive the first challenges to their commitment because they never experienced the new birth at all. It is not that such 'Christians' lack true commitment but that they have never known true conversion.

Many evangelical churches will find that they are more popular than ever before in the postmodern world. But our response should be cautious toward this numerical success. Otherwise we will devote our lives to chasing untameable goats which pass through our midst rather than shepherding God's sheep who have made their home in God's Church.

Three

Virtual Reality: Actual Tragedy

Some years ago I went with a group of friends to Italy for a camping holiday. We were all Christian workers on low incomes and so we decided to drive without making an overnight stay in France. Twenty-four hours after getting off the cross-channel ferry we stopped in an Alpine pass to watch a spectacular sunrise. The scene was breathtaking as the colours and forms of that beautiful landscape unfolded before us. Instinctively we separated from each other to spend time alone with the God who had made such a creation, and when we returned to the car we sat silently for a while.

When it became emotionally possible to talk again we began to recount to each other our feelings and thoughts. One of us exclaimed, 'It was like a scene from a film!' At first we all agreed but then someone replied, 'Wait a minute. That's all wrong. We shouldn't compare reality with illusion. It should be the other way round. A scene in a film might be praised for being realistic but not the real for being like a film. That makes the test of reality the degree to which it conforms to our imagination.'

That is what virtual reality means. The real world is less attractive and less significant than a world of images. That holiday took place twenty years ago, before computer technology became widespread. The only virtual reality we had then was through television and films. Yet even that was enough to make us view real life as second best to an imaginary one. Who hasn't imagined being a character in a film scene? Who hasn't 'replayed' a real conversation which didn't go well, altering the dialogue to make it sound better? Say you have a confrontation with your boss at work in which he or she speaks unfairly and humiliates you. You spend the rest of the day thinking about what you should have said to put them right. By the time you get home to tell your spouse or friends about it you have rewritten the script to your advantage.

Advertisers know the power of such things. They show a cool, elegant woman or man at the wheel of a new car being admired and envied by onlookers. The image becomes you as you will appear if you buy it. Over the generations since film has been invented, self-image has been profoundly influenced by this process. We imagine what we would like to be and then strive to become like the image. It is a process which is used to sell everything, from the drinks we buy to the coffin we are buried or cremated in. It makes us slaves to unreality.

God made us an incredible assortment of shapes and sizes, but films present successful people as uniformly slim and beautiful. God made each one of us unique in our combination of personality, intelligence, looks and temperament, but we pursue impossible dreams of perfect bodies and minds. Human nature is impossibly flawed by sin but we persuade ourselves we can learn to behave without faults. The result is misery, self-hatred, broken dreams of marital bliss and the constant rejection of those who fail us, as they inevitably will. One consequence of this shift from reality to image is the decline of marriage. People who imagine themselves free of complications do not like hard reality. Some can even live their lives with TV screens for company and cease to want real relationships.

The advent of computer technology has weakened our grasp of reality even further. It has become possible to play interactive computer games where the player becomes a character in imaginary worlds. We can escape into another 'reality' with supernatural powers, physical superiority or absolute control over our destiny. It is a frightening trend, especially for young people who have yet to develop their self-awareness and social skills.

The Growth of Fiction

How have we come to this state of things? The answer is in the growth of fiction. Until the sixteenth century there was very little. Then came the playhouse. It was certainly not as respectable as one might imagine from reading Shakespeare now, but at least it was originally 'high art' involving profound moral and social comment. Enlightenment society in its liberalism allowed the increase of fiction writing and bawdy entertainment. Fiction became an increasingly familiar part of people's lives. The addiction of our society to escaping from reality had begun. By the twentieth century, fiction was established as a part of respectable and normal life. Then came radio and film.

Radio brought the first virtual reality into our homes at the turn of a dial. It may be hard to imagine, but the effect was as powerful as virtual reality is now. On one famous occasion before the Second World War, America went into panic over a supposed Martian invasion because Orson Welles broadcast a dramatization of the H.G. Wells story *The War of The Worlds* on radio and masses of people thought it was a news report.

Film was even more powerful, but was originally silent. A breakthrough in technology came in the twenties with the Al Jolson film *The Jazz Singer* which brought together sound and pictures successfully for the first time. The thirties introduced television broadcasting and after the war it spread rapidly. Its effect has been incalculable as a means of escape and as a killer of traditional human values. Needless to say, the original high moral standards of British television have been abandoned so that TV now brings utter filth into the most morally careful home. But in terms of producing our escapist society it is another effect of TV which matters even more.

When I was a boy I spent hour upon hour with friends in role-play games like 'Cowboys and Indians' or imaginative activities with toys as props. They were important experiences in socializing and bonding together. We learned the limits of acceptable behaviour, tested our intelligence and strength in comparison with others, found out how to be caring and forgiving. Children today are discouraged from playing outside due to both the dangers of traffic and of 'something bad' happening to them.

As a result, the first independent and powerful relationship they develop is sexual. It is no wonder that children have 'lost their innocence'. They are perfectly capable of arriving at puberty without any skills and discernment in relationships at all. Starved of peer group contact outside organized activities, the sexual drive of adolescence becomes the button which is inevitably pressed in the search for human closeness independent of family and authority. Those childhood games are replaced by sexual ones in the process of learning self-awareness and identity. Yet there is even worse to come as we approach the new century.

The latest development in computer games is the 'virtual-reality machine' – you wear a headset, which displays a computer generated scene, and a glove which is connected to the computer so that you physically engage to change the scene as if it was real. So far the technology is crude and inefficient. But within a few years, it is predicted, it will be technically possible to have lasting virtual relationships – including sexual ones. The prospect is awful. It could lead to the dehumanization of humanity.

The Loss of Self-identity

The primary victim in the world of virtual reality is the self. It is no longer clear what a human being is and what significance there is in being alive. Once we escaped from reality through someone else's written fiction. With film and radio the process was extended. Now we can live through our own computer generated fiction which we can adapt for ourselves. The boundaries between reality and pretence are virtually wiped out so that we are no more able to understand ourselves as real people than as visual images. Even without playing games, the screen has become ever present in our lives, more a door than a window into escapism and unreality.

This is why today people do not value themselves. It is not just a question of choosing not to. It is that we don't know how to do it. We have lost the tools for the job and like children we stick together ideas of ourselves rather than building self-identity out of real experiences in the way previous generations could. Our cardboard cut-outs cannot survive the knocks of real life. The result is purposeless living: indifference to priorities like meaning in life, fulfilment, loyalty and self-discipline. The end product is indifference, despair, depression and suicide. Life imitates art. The only things which motivate the virtual-reality generation come from life as a pleasurable game both at work and home. Our generation is on a journey to nowhere in terms of self-understanding.

Work is changing because of these trends. It is both more important and less important than before. The Christian view of work is that it is one of the four great vocations alongside family, society and church. God calls us first to worship, then to love, then to work, then to live public lives. The modern world ignores everything which is demanding. Public life is abandoned for the pursuit of individual satisfaction. Love is temporary. Worship is at best optional. Work is a means to two ends: earning money for pleasure, and personal fulfilment. You see this in church life. There is work to be done, but it is sacrificial and tedious. People won't do it because they say, 'I don't feel it would be very fulfilling for me.' The idea of fulfilling the good of the church or of glorifying God has slipped off the agenda.

In previous generations work was about providing for survival, contributing to society and living a well-ordered life. For the Christian, work was above all the service of God. That supreme aim has been lost in the post-Christian, postmodern world. In that sense work is less important. But in another sense it is more important. When work was scarce and salaries low, work was a means of providing for family and personal need. A young person would give most of his or her salary to the family and keep only a small amount for personal use. Today, young people expect to keep most of their income for themselves and pay little or even nothing to parents for board and lodging. If a job is unfulfilling it is felt to be wrong. Work is about personal pleasure and satisfaction. Home becomes the place where you sleep for the night if you don't get a better offer.

Leisure has become the main reason for work. We work to live, and in the postmodern world we live at weekends. The leisure industry has grown out of all proportions in our society, with an endless offer of thrills and pleasures. The line between moral and immoral is completely blurred. Is a massage for health or sexual stimulation? Is a film for entertainment or voyeurism? Is a dance for exercise and fun or for taking ecstacy and sexual intercourse in equal doses? Have we had too much to drink when we cannot think clearly or when we have stopped thinking at all? Plenty of people who see themselves as decent leave their decency outside the door of pleasure 'as long as it doesn't harm someone else'. It is an attitude which is corrupting the Christian Church as young people believe one thing on Saturday night and another on Sunday morning. Sooner or later Sunday morning is cancelled either by non-attendance at church or the demand that church ceases to be invasive of personal and private choice. Those who keep coming anyway begin to see church and God as necessary guilt trips to clean up our act before Monday when we begin the slide through our week all over again.

Counselling services have risen in popularity as the inevitable result of such a way of life. When people have lost the meaning of life they need help. It is not the crises of bereavement or divorce which produce most counselling clients but the desire to understand, to accept and to change ourselves. I have counselled thousands of students during my years of involvement in higher education. The cases of traumatic crisis are comparatively few. The search for self has been my more usual agenda. It is inevitable when our society has drifted away from reality into the cardboard cut-out approach to self-image. As presenters on Blue Peter say, people when they go to counsellors say of their self-understanding, 'here's one I made earlier'.

In the world of virtual reality, there is another tragic but inevitable consequence. It is an addictive world where drugs soften the blow of harsh reality whenever it intrudes on our self-image. Alcohol, cannabis and Prozac provide feelings of self-ease. The harder drugs open another door – the general anaesthetic of total illusion instead of the local one of drink and pills. We must be careful what we condemn, of course. Alcohol is not in itself an evil and neither are tranquilizers. Neither pleasure nor relief from inner conflict are sins. But the addictive society does not wait for such legitimate moments. The aim is neither serious nor cautious but simply one of immediate self-indulgence. Life without pleasure is non-existence and therefore pleasure is king. Even when the pleasure kills, as in drugs which bring about fatal illnesses, like heroin or the habitual use of nicotine. The world of virtual reality is the world of unreality. It is a world without consequences, even though the consequences are perfectly clear.

That is the fundamental problem. Virtual reality eliminates unpleasant consequences. In a computer game you can be killed and start the game again. You can play with demons and switch off the screen afterwards. It mirrors real dilemmas of life and leads us to believe we can divorce and not feel pain, or abandon our responsibilities and have no difficulty. You can, in effect, be immoral and still be a decent person.

The consequences of this for Christianity are both positive and negative. Positively, Christianity can be a light in the darkness, a place where lost people can find God and themselves, learn how to love, base their lives on the sure Word of God and live for the highest of purposes and greatest of pleasures. Negatively, we run the risk of being moulded into the world we live in. Conversion becomes a temporary pleasure, like drugs. The Bible becomes an encumbrance to 'meaningful faith'. The church becomes driven by the need to entertain.

If we are to survive and succeed we must recapture the biblical meanings of conversion, discipleship truth and fellowship.

Four

What is a Dad? Or a Mum? – or for that matter any kind of lasting relationship with a real person?

Have you heard of children divorcing their parents? It is a new idea in social law but it has been suggested both in America and Britain. It has actually been tried in the American legal system so it is more than just a theory.

What lies behind this tragedy is the fact that young people today increasingly feel unwelcome in their own homes. In Britain homelessness has grown steadily throughout the eighties and nineties and the main source of the problem is teenagers who abandon their family ties. Even if they do not physically leave, children are showing many signs of rejecting their parents' interest in them and authority over them. It is vital to understand what is going on here.

Authority that has Lost its Authority

One of the primary problems is that authority has lost its authority. Throughout the Christian era authority has been regarded as God-ordained and subject to his law. In the last chapter I mentioned the four Christian callings of church, family, public life and work. Each of them carried the responsibility of submitting to a higher authority ordained by God. In church there was the presiding minister or elder. In family life there was the headship of the father. In public life there was the properly recognized government, whether inherited or democratic. In work there was the employer.

Each of these authorities is capable of being delegated. The minister has fellow leaders, the father shares his role with his wife, government appoints representatives and law officers while employers choose supervisors and managers to act on their behalf. Furthermore, each of these authorities is subject to biblical and moral restraint. Church leaders must show wisdom and compassion. Governments are required to be impartial in justice and protective of their subjects. Parents should be loving and gentle. Employers are to be just and fair in their treatment of workers.

The ultimate tribunal for neglect and failure was the judgement of God both in this life and the life to come. I say 'was' not because I do not believe it is true now but because people widely believed in it until the Age of Enlightenment and have steadily rejected it since. The end result is our own generation which regards all religious beliefs as nothing but ideas and therefore unreal. That is the fundamental reason why law and order, commitment to justice, personal honesty and so forth have been abandoned in these areas. There has been a great deal of attention to this loss of commitment to good authority, but the effect on family life is neglected.

For thousands of years British family life has been established on the natural relationships of parents to children and on the Christian teaching that family is God-ordained. Divorce and desertion were extremely uncommon before this century so that the 'natural' order of things was seldom undermined. Three factors in particular have conspired against the Christian order: rejection of Christian values, women's rights and divorce.

The Rejection of Christian Values

Long before Christianity became publicly rejected in Britain, there was a decline in Christian teaching. The eighteenth-century church was politically powerful but spiritually bankrupt. Only the evangelical revival prevented a complete débâcle for British Christianity then. But evangelicalism, as we have noted, lost its focus on the wider implications of biblical faith as it pursued individual conversion and discipleship. The individual displaced the church as the focal point of Christian living.

The next generation of evangelicals after Wesley and Whitefield saw the need for addressing societal problems and brought about a great improvement in public life. Leading figures such as William Wilberforce and Lord Shaftesbury devoted themselves to eradicating public evils like slavery, child exploitation, bad working conditions and slum housing. They also developed prison and poor law reform and care for the mentally ill. They were widely supported by evangelical churches who also added their growing influence in the nineteenth century to overtly religious campaigns such as religious liberty. The chapels had their own agenda and fought for religious equality, universal education free of Anglican bias and the abolition of Anglican credal tests for university entrance.

Few people realize how much our modern world has been shaped by these evangelical campaigns for social justice and family values. Their success, reinforced by the growth of evangelical churches and chapels throughout the century, was marked by the development of a British conscience and way of life centred on the family and the church. Even as late as the 1950s the British Sunday, established by Victorian society, was regarded by Winston Churchill as a national institution essential for the well-being of family and society.

But the fifties actually delivered the death-blow to Victorian values. It was the era of post-war freedom and materialism, the development of the teenage culture of rock and roll, the rise of TV and mass advertising and many other assaults on Christian attitudes to life. It is unfair to blame one generation, but that particular one did open the door wide to the secular society which mushroomed in the sixties and in which we now live.

The Changing Role of Women

As well as our rejection of Christian values for the family a more specific issue has been enormously influential over family life: the changing role of women. The biblical view of the home is that the father is head and the main provider of material things, while the wife is his helpmeet and the main provider of close family relationships. Proverbs chapter 31 makes clear that the 'good wife' was to be highly respected both within the family and the community and was by no means meant to be a doormat without economic or social status. But the Christian Church allowed a great abuse of these principles by tolerating the misuse of authority by men and their degrading of women into little more than domestic slaves.

When biblical knowledge was widespread and respected this balance was maintained, at least by believing families. With the decline of Christian faith and of respect for authority, women have turned to other ideologies for their self-worth and indeed have rightly seized their opportunity to recover self-respect and economic security. That opportunity came supremely in wartime when the men were absent and women proved they could do as much as men in the offices and factories. After the war there was no returning to 'wifey at home and hubby at work'. Nor was there any returning to the unchallenged authority of men in the home. Women – and children for that matter – had survived without men for five years of war, and the men returned to find a new and less certain place in the family home.

The feminist movement became the primary voice of women. No one should doubt that there is justice in the call for women to be treated as professionally equal with men. But feminism has frequently presented being equal as being identical, apart from physical gender. Extreme feminists have sometimes even advocated lesbian rather than heterosexual relationships in order for women to become completely independent of men.

As a result, the Christian emphasis on complementarity between man and woman has been lost. In the world of work this loss is noticeable rather than tragic. In the world of family life it is tragic in the extreme. It has influenced a generation of children already who do not have an explanation for the real differences between male and female, yet who have to live with these in practice because some differences are inherent rather than merely inherited by role modelling.

The effect on family life is that authority has been lost. No one figure is universally regarded as the family head. As a result, children are not disciplined in the proper sense of the word. Discipline is not primarily a question of smacking or removing privileges for bad behaviour. It is first of all the process of establishing a sense of order in the home. Order provides stability and security. When parents do not know how to complement each other they compete with each other for dominance instead. The real loss in that is the loss of a stable order, experienced not only by the children of one home but by children in general. It is an ideological vacuum in our society that we have no agreed model for the family. Even the feminist movement has declined in power in this postmodern atmosphere of suspicion against every form of ideology.

The Rising Divorce Rate

Another onslaught against Christian values in the home has come through the rising divorce rate in Britain. There has been a terrible loss of love in modern society. People today think of love as romance and passion. Christianity has a view of love, as well as of marriage, which places mutual respect and sacrificial service before feelings. Those virtues have been abandoned in favour of the personal quest for stability between two 'equals'. It has become much harder for our society to agree on what respect is due to a husband and a wife and therefore to a father and mother. When respect and stability are lacking, love will be unpredictable as well. Parents do fall in and out of love through the course of a long marriage. Divorce is an easy option when we hit a bad patch. The message we give to children then is that love is not unconditional and that their needs are second to our own as parents.

The obvious consequence is that children will not express unconditional love either. They will protect themselves against the threat of insecurity and rejection and what is more they will give only as much respect as they see in (and experience from) their parents. My youngest child is called Abigail, a Hebrew name which means 'Father's joy'. She and her father take her name very seriously. Yet even she has said to me from time to time, 'Daddy, you and Mummy will never divorce, will you?' She sees so many of her friends lose a parent through divorce and she brings into our home the pain she has felt for them. She does not want to be reassured that I love her. She knows her name! What she does want is the reassurance that my love for my wife is unconditional and stable. We reap what we sow with a vengeance in this department of life.

Marriages are not loveless when parents do not feel emotion for each other. They are loveless when parents do not ensure that they maintain friendship, respect and support in the long term. If those values are firmly in place, love will follow. It is the neglect of these principles that is causing the high rate of divorce today. Loveless marriages produce inadequate bases for bringing up children long before they become broken marriages.

Another consequence of modern marriage is the loss of parenting skills. In the Christian faith, the father as head of the home is the primary disciplinarian and teacher. The mother is the primary carer who provides a loving and secure environment. These are not absolute, of course. The mother may share in discipline and teaching and the father should certainly share in the task of loving and nurturing children. But the roles need to be clearly delineated to the children so that they receive clear models for their own identities as male and female. Equal human worth for man and woman is communicated through mutual respect and love, not identical actions and behaviour.

Once again, our modern society has lost its way. The mother is seen as the primary religious leader in the home and often the primary disciplinarian. Dad is too often late home from work or out with his 'mates'. In homes where both parents work the situation is getting completely out of hand. Parents increasingly provide substitute parents when the children are too young to go to school and absent themselves completely from their roles at the most formative period of a child's self-understanding.

When school age is reached, parents expect the impossible – that schools can replace the home as the place where good behaviour is taught. That is both morally wrong and ideologically dangerous. There is no one moral agenda agreed by teachers before they enter their profession, nor do they have the means to enforce one. That is why expulsions are becoming more common. Teachers cannot use physical punishment in an age which labels it cruel (which it is not necessarily). They cannot use detention when children have to catch buses to distant homes. Extra work becomes less effective when homework is becoming essential to the fulfilment of normal educational programmes. Most fundamental of all, they cannot impose their authority when respect for authority is at an end in our world.

The loss of clear parenting roles means that children do not develop the appropriate childhood skills of respect for wider authority and people other than their own. The result is that children turn to 'tribal' behaviour with others of their own age. Instead of the home providing security and stability, these are provided by the gang. Even the children of stable homes get sucked into this tribal culture of young people today because it has become so universal. You cannot go out after school hours without seeing a group of sometimes very young children hanging about shopping areas and street corners. Often they get up to mischief of some kind because hanging around is boring and being in a group gives them a power they should not have. The government talks about introducing punishments for 'bad' parents when their children misbehave in public. But what is the effect going to be when there is no corresponding agenda for good parenting? The problem is not simply that individual parents neglect their responsibilities so much as that no one is prepared to say what those responsibilities are. That is the point we have reached in our society.

So far, we have only analysed the crisis in relationships from the perspective of what comes out of the home. However, the dilemma is much worse. The prevailing attitudes of society inevitably creep into the best of homes, through TV and video, through the example of other families we know and most of all through the peer group pressure of society as a whole.

We have seen how family life is breaking down completely. It will not stop there. Crime and lawlessness will increase as respect for home, public life and employers decreases. It is already obvious in the growing crime rate among young people. Most crimes are now committed by people under twenty-five. These young offenders used to be almost exclusively male but that is changing as well. It may be that Christians need to start a campaign for changes in the education system so that Christian schools can be established out of tax money to reflect our particular facet of the multi-faith society in which we now live. At least then we will be able to influence large numbers of young people with Christian moral values. Christians have a ready ally for educational reform in Islam, because the Islamic community is as concerned as – perhaps more concerned than – the Christian Church about these trends.

The next generation is crucial. The divorce rate will escalate further as children grow up untaught in good family practice and all too well instructed in the temporary nature of their parents' marriages. We are heading for either total breakdown in British society or a new religious era when something fills the vacuum left by the loss of Christian values. Other religionists know this. Does the Christian Church realize how crucial a time it is?

Five

Who Moved My Stone?

Some years ago a lawyer by the name of Frank Morrison decided to write an exposé of the resurrection of Christ entitled *Who Moved the Stone?* He was a convinced unbeliever and realized that if the resurrection were proved to be a hoax or a delusion then Christianity could not claim to be true. Being a good lawyer, he investigated the story as carefully as he could. The result was his conversion to the Christian faith. The book caused quite a stir when it was published in the inter-war period and helped many sceptics in their quest for truth.

A different story illustrates the search for religious certainty today. I used to teach a counselling skills course at a college in Swansea. One day, a student became very agitated after the ten minute break. She was a 'New Age' type, inseparable from a string of what I thought were beads which she wore round her neck. Her distress was caused by the fact that she couldn't find them. 'Who moved my stones?' she asked. 'I need them for my spiritual energy.' Her contrasting question illustrates the change from old religion to new in the postmodern age.

Truth does not matter in the new spirituality. Maybe Jesus did rise from the dead. After all, the world is full of spiritual mysteries. The question is, does believing in him help me to find inner transquillity and strength? If it does, Christianity is for me. If not, I can try any of the other spiritual voices and powers, from Satan to sacred stones around my neck. No one has a right to deny me my personal choice and no one has the right to criticize the one I make.

I shall always remember one particular religious debate I had with a friend. I spent several hours with him as I unfolded the gospel story. When we turned to the subject of sin I explained that God would judge each one of us according to our decision to accept or reject Jesus Christ as Saviour. He was not religious himself, but he ended our discussion abruptly with the words, 'My God would never do that.' Until then I had not realized, and he had not revealed, that he 'had' a God at all. In fact, he had one of his own construction and imagination. That is New Age spirituality. A pick-and-mix religion where you choose for yourself what kind of religion or God you want and reject any challenge to it on the basis that you personally do not accept it.

New Age Spirituality

The respectability of New Age spirituality is well established in Britain. There are one or two astrologers, for example, whose services are sought after by the most famous people in Britain, including the late and much lamented Princess Diana, according to news reports before her death. The fact that she had a Christian funeral perfectly illustrates New Age attitudes. No one spiritual direction need exclude another.

Where does this new concern for spiritual reality come from? It seems very odd that only a generation ago religion was almost totally rejected in favour of 'scientific facts' and rational certainties about this world.

First of all, we have to realize just how deep the religious instinct is in humanity. There is not one single culture or society which does not have a religion. It is both endemic and epidemic in human existence. Sociologists may say that the instinct is produced by human uncertainty about life and death, but the strange thing is that our own culture had just about explained every 'gap' in our understanding of life. Yet it has not lessened religious feeling but increased it. The religions which derive from the Old and New Testaments have another explanation. God created us for himself and without him we are conscious of something missing. There is a God-shaped hole in the human heart which only he can fill. That is why our technological, scientific, sceptical age has not eradicated religious belief but actually increased it. The more people are offered alternatives the more those alternatives are seen to be inadequate.

That does not explain how people are turning to self-made religion, however. The explanation for that lies in the history of our age.

In the first place, Christianity has been subjected to almost limitless abuse and ridicule in recent years and appears to many people to be totally discredited. No other religion is as self-critical as Christian faith. Some of that criticism appears to be self-destructive as so-called leaders deny such fundamental truths as the authority of Scripture, the divinity of Christ and his bodily resurrection. But even worse than considered arguments, which can at least be countered, is the ridicule and abuse allowed in the media. They may be very careful not to insult other religions, but when it comes to Christianity there is an open season. Clergy are presented as fools and hypocrites. Christians are presented as naïve. God and Christ are blasphemed against freely. It is no wonder that traditional Christianity is rejected by so many today. Christianity has lost the battle for public credibility.

Secondly, there is a well established critique of religion which reappears in several academic disciplines, notably the philosophy of religion. Typically, the analysis of religion presented is that all belief systems share certain characteristics in outlook or experience. Then the conclusion is offered that all religions are therefore essentially the same and are man-made. In fact, the conclusion is unwarranted from the facts and is inaccurate in the extreme. The possibility is ruled out by sceptics from the outset that a God exists who has revealed himself. But the argument further ignores how much the main world religions differ fundamentally in all sorts of ways. Nevertheless the idea has gained both academic and popular respectability. It has added to the momentum against traditional Christian faith and worship.

Thirdly, we live in a what has come to be known as 'the global village'. We are much more aware of other cultures and beliefs than a few generations ago was even possible. Britain itself is a multi-faith society in a minor way, in that a small percentage of the population comes from other faith communities such as Judaism, Islam, Hinduism and Buddhism. This multi-faith dimension of British society has sometimes been exaggerated (the number of churches far exceeds the total of all other places of worship added together), but it is nevertheless significant enough to make us all aware of other religions being practised within the population. As a result, Christianity does not have the same respect it had as recently as in our grandparents' generation.

Another factor is the death of truth. When you mentioned science twenty or thirty years ago people would almost automatically think of the word 'proof'. 'Science has proved' was a phrase as sacred to some as 'God is love' is to Christians. In the postmodern world people have stopped saying 'science has proved' and are more likely to think 'science has destroyed'. Science (and its twin brother technology) has certainly interfered with the balance of nature, causing catastrophic damage to such things as the ozone layer, green forests, the blue whale, and for all we know the future of humanity. Scientific truth has become suspect because if has allowed us to invent mass destruction, poison the food chain and threaten species of life, including our own.

Truth has therefore been 'executed' by the postmodern world. The death of scientific truth has undermined all claims to truth, whether scientific, political, philosophical or religious. The idea that any one religion is true seems arrogant today. The very idea that religion is about truth has become meaningless in the new spirituality. The new 'truth' of religion is experiential. The ideas do not matter very much compared with whether the religion followed delivers a meaningful experience which enables people to understand and somehow control an increasingly confusing and mysterious world of reality.

Finally, what the new spirituality itself means by 'spiritual experience' needs to be carefully understood. The Christian means by that an experience of Jesus Christ which leads to lasting fellowship with God. A similar kind of claim is made for spiritual experience in Judaism and Islam. But the model for spiritual experience today does not come from those sources so much as from eastern religions. The experience which attracts people today is that of mystery and inner reality. I hope I can explain those two dimensions.

New age mystery

The new spirituality believes in a haunted universe with many sources of spiritual reality. That is why occult practices such as astrology and spiritualism are as easily accepted as Christian ones which lead to Christ. Indeed, they are regarded as essentially the same, since all spirituality is accepted as the same benevolent thing. The *Daily Mail* of 7 November 1997 illustrates the total confusion caused by this idea. It carried a two-page spread entitled 'Charlie's Angel' which began, 'Everyone has a guardian angel, according to Elsa Ayling.' Ayling is a spiritualist who practises 'psychic art'. She drew pictures of these 'guardian angels' – which are actually mediumistic spirit guides – which she attributed to several famous people, including the strongly Catholic wife of our current prime minister.

None of the guardians were angelic. All were people who had supposedly lived in previous generations. Some of them were nuns who, if real, would probably have rejected such practices as witchcraft, but no such niceties of fact intrude on the world of new spirituality. They did not intrude on the *Daily Mail*, either, which made no attempt at critical or even impartial reporting. The test offered of this psychic's view of reality was simply whether she could produce what she offered. No comment about these spirits was made, not even whether some were malevolent rather than helpful. All that mattered was entering into the world of spiritual forces. That is what the New Age spirituality means by 'mystery'.

New age inner reality

My second description of new age spirituality is that it is focused on inner reality. Christians use the term 'spiritual experience' to describe an experience either of God or evil. The new spirituality has its focus on the self. Spiritual means 'having a spiritual dimension in oneself'. The difference is this. Christian experience leads to people serving God. New spiritual experience leads to spiritual powers serving us. They are there to make us feel better about ourselves, to be more in touch with the whole of human reality, to be more fulfilled, to be more at peace, to be more powerful.

Is it spirituality? Sometimes real (not necessarily good) powers are touched. Sometimes it is nothing more than emotion which cannot easily be explained. The Christian faith has two explanations which need to be taken much more seriously than they are. First, human life is itself spiritual as well as material. There is indeed something more to us than merely physical and emotional existence. Second, the devil began his war against us by promising to serve us (Gen. 3). It is an old lie that still works and that is what many people are experiencing in their spiritual search.

At the same time, God is merciful and does use this spiritual hunger to lead people to himself. New age spirituality is not something we should automatically reject, therefore. It raises important questions about human spirituality which we have no right to ignore. The most fundamental is the nature of true spiritual experience. I have said that evangelicalism has been profoundly influenced by the Enlightenment. Two aspects of spirituality have been made more confusing as a result. I can illustrate what I mean with the famous Bible verse 'God is love.'

First, 'God is love' involves an idea about God. God has revealed himself through ideas. That is what Scripture largely consists of. The Enlightenment was very positive toward intellectual ideas, but it was wrong to believe that ideas contain the whole truth. 'God is love' is more than an idea. It is a real description of God's real nature. You cannot say that you prefer to believe 'God is hate' because it conforms to your experience. The idea is non-negotiable. Whatever your experience says about God, his revelation in Scripture stands above you.

But secondly, 'God is love' promises an experience. The Enlightenment did not like that at all. It distrusted experience and especially any experience which smacked of emotionalism. That is why the Methodist revival was branded as 'enthusiasm'. It was as good an insult as the Enlightenment could manage with its hatred of personal, subjective emotions. Unfortunately, evangelicalism has a long history of doing the same thing. Emotion has been banned from public worship and has been suspect in private devotions. Emotion in worship was banished in the name of 'order', which really meant 'keep to ideas'. Emotion in private prayer was belittled in favour of Bible study and a 'Prayer List'. Jacob's cry, 'I will not let you go unless you bless me' was replaced for many evangelicals with the bland assumption that 'I have had my Quiet Time so I must be blessed whether I know it or not.' I believe and I do the right thing. That is the heart of much evangelical life.

The new spirituality is an indictment both of Enlightenment ideas of people and of the unbalanced message of the evangelical church. Human experience is emotional as well as volitional and intellectual. And biblical spirituality involves feeling as well as choice and belief. Indeed, true spirituality is not something we do but something God does within us. The Holy Spirit works within the believer, producing in us both the will and the desire to please God (Phil. 2:13) and an inner experience which is more than emotion itself (Rom. 8:15, 16). Recent evangelical life has been deeply influenced by charismatic spirituality and you can see why. Here is a model of spiritual experience which gives full recognition to emotional experience. But the truth lies in between the old and this new kind of evangelicalism. Experience does not equal emotion any more than it excludes it. We shall look again at this issue later in more detail.

Part Two

The Church In Its Image

Six

Unity Without Truth

Some years ago I was honorary Baptist Chaplain to Swansea University. As a convinced and very conservative evangelical I wondered how I would relate to my Roman Catholic counterpart, an ultra-conservative priest who regarded modern Catholicism with some disdain. To our mutual surprise we found ourselves drawn to each other in close friendship and genuine fellowship. We shared much in common both in doctrine and moral vision. We recognized Christ in each other and welcomed it. But we had fundamental differences as well. He believed Christ was in me because of my baptism while I believed Christ was in him because of his faith!

Between us we agreed an agenda for our work which did not compromise our respective convictions or lead others to suppose we shared the same ones. What we did share was a united front for the honour of Christ in the university and in addressing the moral mess of student life. But we were both criticized by others who felt that if we saw Christ in each other that was enough.

The dividing line was drawn between us and those who said that experience was all important. That sounds like a spiritual statement, but in fact it comes from the heart of postmodernism. Truth is no longer the focus for agreement: experience is.

The postmodern world does not value truth. Truth has become one person's perspective, a collection of subjective and fallible ideas about the reality which is greater than all ideas. Two consequences flow from that belief. The first is that certainty is seen as arrogance. The second is that conflicting ideas should be welcomed as contributions to the search for meaning. These attitudes have become very influential, and have crept into evangelical life.

Certainty is Arrogant

Evangelical Christianity is essentially based on the belief that God has spoken through his Word and therefore his Word in Scripture is binding upon the mind and heart. It is a claim to certainty. That does not mean that we will always agree about matters of interpretation, but it does mean that our view of truth is not negotiable. We may agree to differ with those who receive the Scriptures as God's truth but who interpret it differently. But we cannot agree to differ with those who seek to alter or undermine that authority in some fundamental way.

Throughout the history of Christianity there have been two ways in which Scripture has been undermined. Some have subtracted from the truth by refusing to accept what the Bible teaches, while others have added to the truth by acknowledging further revelations. Virtually the whole story of 'heresy' – false beliefs within the church – has been told when these two trends are acknowledged. Modern evangelicalism does not know its Bible, especially the doctrines taught by it. As a result we are losing our ability to discern when heresy is being taught. Does it matter? History shows how much can be lost by either subtracting from or adding to the Word of God.

Subtracting from the truth of the Bible

The route of subtraction has mainly been a Protestant one. The reason for this change is largely the influence of rationalism on evangelical belief. Rationalism has placed reason above Scripture so that if something goes against the current mood or the opinion of society's intellectual élite it tends to be rejected.

The primary example of subtraction is liberal Christianity, which began as an attempt to reconcile evangelical belief with the world of the Enlightenment. It was based on the assumption that the Bible is a product of its own writers to the extent that some of its teachings are not divinely revealed but are only accidental expressions of a writer's own mind or of the society in which that writer lived. The test of truth became what was credible to the believer.

It must be said that evangelical theologians have never been unwilling to recognize the human element in Scripture. The disagreement has not been about that fact, but rather about what consequences flow from the human dimension of Scripture. The evangelical position is that God used the human element to fulfil his purpose while the more liberal theologians have argued that it must have obscured the divine revelation. It is important to note this distinction because liberal opponents frequently have failed to notice it. Conservative theology has been unfairly represented by its opponents by taking the writings of ill-informed people as representative of the whole.

For example, Calvin has remained a standard authority among conservative evangelical theologians and he frequently commented on apparent discrepancies, the different emphases of one writer over another in Scripture and even about whether some passages found in our Bible were original or additions which crept in at a later stage. The human dimension of Scripture is real and of great significance in understanding the Bible. Where the battle line has been drawn is over such things as whether the miraculous was an invention or real, whether the human dimension introduced a loss of God's original Word, whether we can trust the Scriptures in areas about which it is clear in its intention. Rejecting the dependability of the Bible allowed liberals to reconstruct the New Testament faith and claim that it was really exactly what the rationalists had 'discovered' many centuries later.

The most devastating aspect of this idea was the fact that Enlightenment intellectuals did not believe in the miraculous. Consequently, the very basis of Christian faith in biblical revelation was challenged. The Bible came to be seen as a human product. Its accounts of miraculous events, from the Flood to the resurrection, were placed in doubt. Instead, Christianity was presented by many as a religious ideal supremely developed by the life and teaching of Jesus, who was 'a moral master' rather than the divine Son of God. The Jesus of liberalism was really a good Enlightenment man!

Ever since that concept of Christian truth has developed, there has been a constant trend to explain away divine revelation in word and deed. The virgin birth is seen as an ancient idea rather than a fact of history. The cross is an example of suffering rather than a real act of atonement for sin. The resurrection is a spiritual truth rather than a physical event. The healings of the Bible are stories to illustrate Jesus' status rather than actual reversals of the natural order. The disciples may have believed in them, but the 'rational person' knows that such things do not happen.

Liberal Christianity thrived within the institutions of the Protestant churches, especially among denominational leaders and theological teachers. It is largely a spent force in churches today, partly because evangelicals have become more scholarly and have become expert at dealing with the arguments put forward by liberalism. It used to seem that uneducated Christians believed in the Bible while educated people saw through this naïve approach. That is no longer a credible attack on traditional beliefs.

Furthermore, the basis of liberalism has been undermined by postmodernism, with its firm rejection of the rationalistic outlook of the Enlightenment. Liberals put forward ideas based on rationalist doubts about the supernatural, but the postmodern world believes in mystery and supernatural realities with ease. However, the liberal movement is moving on to postmodern ideas itself. Now there are theologians who base their studies on the idea that all certainty is arrogant, that all perspectives are to be welcomed and that Jesus is one of several 'spiritual figures' to be revered.

The process is clearly seen in world ecumenism. The ecumenical movement began as an experiment in co-operation for world mission. Then the vision for reunification took pride of place. Liberal Christians came to the fore in this movement. They tended to be in leadership of the Protestant denominations and had much in common with each other. They were also the theologians most willing to question the value of holding to those distinctive interpretations of the Bible which have divided Christians over the years. As liberalism has declined, postmodern emphases have taken its place in world ecumenism.

This has been vividly illustrated in recent world ecumenical events, where worship has included forms of 'spirituality' that differ from even the most liberal Christian ones. British ecumenical co-operation has taken a somewhat different and more orthodox path, as both evangelicals and Roman Catholics have joined its ranks with their concern for traditional Christian beliefs. However, even here the postmodern mood has had an impact because many people do not know or care deeply about details of doctrine and are willing to assume the existence of spiritual unity on very broad terms.

Adding to the authority of Scripture

The other route by which Scripture has been undermined is that of adding to Scripture another authority.

The oldest manifestation of this comes in the form of church tradition. In both the Catholic and Orthodox Churches, tradition has a status alongside Scripture. The logic is understandable. Over the centuries after Jesus there were many great controversies about what was true. Was Jesus, for example, truly human or only apparently born in the flesh? Was he truly divine, or was he in some way influenced specially – perhaps even uniquely – by God? It took a council of church leaders meeting at Nicaea to come to a definite decision which bound the whole ancient church. They produced what we now call the *Nicaean Creed* which asserts that Jesus was truly human and fully divine in one person, the second person of the Trinity.

Other councils decided equally controversial issues which affected the message of the Christian faith. Their decisions became the basis for much of the doctrine we still accept today as 'Orthodox' Christianity. In the 'Catholic' tradition these councils were accorded the same status as Scripture. God was still speaking through his apostles, the bishops and supremely the Pope, as he had spoken during the days of the early Christians.

This idea eventually led to a medieval Church which obscured the actual teachings of Scripture, especially over the way of salvation. The Church became the source of salvation, which was dispensed especially through the sacraments of baptism and the Mass. Personal conversion through repentance and faith in the cross of Christ became replaced by faith in the Church and its sacraments to most devout believers, a doctrine which led to the Reformation and the Protestant rejection of Catholic Church authority.

The Roman Catholic Church regards the Pope as having still the power to speak on behalf of Christ to bind all Christians to his pronouncements. Evangelical Christians have always resisted this claim. They have respected the Councils of the ancient Church but have insisted that their authority is less than Scripture, which stands permanently above any body of Christians. But it is not only Catholicism which has added to the authority of Scripture. Protestantism has its own story of adding new revelations.

Protestants do not believe any one church can claim to have the whole truth absolutely, because that claim must be made only for Jesus Christ as he is revealed in the Old and New Testaments. Furthermore, it is accepted as a fact beyond contradiction that the medieval Church substantially lost its hold on the message of salvation through faith in Christ. Consequently, there is a great tolerance of criticism and debate about what the Bible actually teaches.

The good side of this process is that we do not exalt denominations above their proper status as human ways of organizing the divinely created fellowship of Christian believers. The bad side is that it has provided a charter for all kinds of false and sometimes ridiculous claims to new truths. Usually those claims involve saying that the truth which was lost in medieval Christianity remained lost among the first Protestants and has only recently been rediscovered by some person God has favoured with new revelation.

These sects often produce books of their own which rank alongside the Bible as revelation but in practice render it secondary. The Jehovah Witnesses, the Mormons, the Christian Scientists and until comparatively recently the Seventh Day Adventists, are all the products of this trend and there are others less well-known. There are many devout believers who are led astray by these groups. Their faith in Christ may perhaps be real, but their beliefs about him and the way of salvation are frankly fantastic and often contrary to the plain meaning of the New Testament. Such cults have begun and flourished most in America, which has for centuries had an evangelical movement committed equally to personal study of the Bible and suspicion of 'scholarship'.

The division between scholarly evangelical belief and unorthodox groups began to break down in the twentieth century. Two movements have achieved this unhappy state more than any others.

First, a group of orthodox evangelicals mounted a huge campaign against liberalism in the early part of the century. They produced a series of tracts asserting 'the fundamental truths' such as the virgin birth, the atonement and the physical resurrection of Christ. It was a bitter episode which was originally led by eminent scholars but which became more popularist and made the average evangelical deeply suspicious of modern academic studies in theology. It gave birth to the term 'fundamentalist', a term which has become synonymous with 'anti-intellectual' and 'bigoted'. The label still adheres to evangelical belief despite its original inaccuracy and certainly its current untruthfulness. At the same time it must be admitted that popular evangelicalism is too often indifferent to proper scholarship and careful study of Christian truth. Consequently, in many of our evangelical churches people do approach the Bible with too little concern for its original message and the complex world of truth which it represents.

The second movement which broke down the walls between scholarly traditional evangelical belief and the world of the cults was the emergence of Pentecostalism. Here was a movement which was on the whole orthodox in belief but which preached a new revelation about the Holy Spirit which usually led people to leave 'dead evangelical' churches to enter into the experience of the Holy Spirit. Frequently, it was asserted that evangelicals had the Bible but not the Spirit. Individual leaders were accorded the status of being God's spokesman (or woman). This was a common claim within the cults but not for any evangelical preacher, no matter how famous or successful, because none would have dared to claim it.

Those things in themselves would not have produced additions to the Bible. But the Pentecostal emphasis on modern prophecy and revelation has certainly allowed some (not all by any means) to believe that a word of prophecy is on the same level as Scripture. The result has been for those people to downplay the Bible and its serious study. The charismatic movement has developed from Pentecostal roots and reflects both good and bad Pentecostal practice. The result is that this major (and to my mind God-given) movement has deeply influenced modern evangelicalism away from its older biblical basis.

Evangelicalism has been influenced by all these trends. We are nervous of asserting the authority of Scripture, we are much less interested than in previous generations in knowing the Bible accurately. When Scripture loses its hold on evangelical life, evangelical life is doomed to decay and perish.

All Perspectives are Equal

We turn now to the second consequence for truth of postmodern influence on the evangelical world. Postmodernism believes that all perspectives are equal and none should be disqualified on the basis of being plain wrong. This thinking has crept into evangelical church life as well as a loss of certainty about the place of the Bible.

Evangelicals have the longest history of any Christian movement of co-operating across denominational boundaries. But that tradition was based on regarding some truths as primary and non-negotiable (about the message of salvation) while other truths were secondary even though important for church life (such as baptism or State patronage). Under the influence of postmodernism, evangelicals are less and less able to articulate any distinctive beliefs at all and are therefore beginning to disregard the difference between evangelicals and others.

The uniting force among many modern evangelicals is not doctrine but experience. If people have any kind of experience which is attributed to Jesus then it is likely to be treated as a saving experience of him. If Christians show loyalty to Jesus or openness to the Holy Spirit, that is regarded as enough. Consequently, churches are becoming less based on doctrinal distinctives and more on style or leadership. To the extent that this causes churches to focus more on the biblical message of salvation there is much good achieved. But the inability to recognize heresies, whether of the 'Bible-plus' or the Bible-minus' type, is leading to confusion and the loss rather than the assertion of the evangelical message.

There is a less important but practical problem as well. Is it better for Christians to agree to differ about baptism but commit themselves to words of revelation or to the authority of a particular leader, or is it better to have a clear doctrinal position to which leader and member alike must be committed. I believe passionately in the latter rather than the former. Unity without truth is no unity at all. That is why so much division and suspicion is spoiling the charismatic and evangelical world today.

Seven

Conversion Without God

Evangelicals believe in conversion. We do not simply believe the message of the gospel but claim to have an authentic experience of it through Jesus Christ. Postmodernism resonates with evangelicalism very well at this point because the postmodern world is deeply committed to having experiences which prove the reality of a belief.

But postmodernism welcomes all kinds of experience of the mysterious and even of the self. This love of experience for its own sake has crept into evangelical life. The most blatant points of penetration are in evangelism and worship. Both, of course, have to be relevant and persuasive. But relevant to what and persuasive of what? The gospel is a message addressed first and foremost to the mind and the conscience. The object of evangelism is that people may repent, believe and be saved. Anything which confirms and reinforces that message is to be welcomed. But much modern evangelism and worship is actually addressed not to the mind and the conscience but to the senses and emotions.

A Personal Example

My own conversion illustrates the problem. I was brought up to believe in atheism and socialism by my father, who had been a political street-preacher in his youth. By the age of thirteen I was a convinced unbeliever who saw no purpose in the 'accident of life' caused by evolution. I contemplated suicide as the logical step to take if life has no meaning and no promise of happiness. In the goodness of God my sister was converted at that time and through her I saw the possibility that there was a God after all who just might have a purpose for my life. I began to search for him.

My sister attended a free evangelical church which was a glorified hut with dull features and awful music. As a keen musician I was put off going after one or two visits and decided to join the choir at the local and very beautiful Anglican church instead. It changed my life. Until then I was a tearaway, getting into trouble my parents never knew about and making myself drunk every Saturday. Now I looked forward to church, to singing God's praise, to learning the ancient prayers of the services and even to preparing for confirmation. I still got drunk on Saturdays but my life settled down a great deal.

After some months my sister asked me if I had been converted. I was indignant with her. Couldn't she see that I had changed, that I had improved my lifestyle, that I looked forward to Sundays more than any other day? Yes, she could. But she did not think I had found Christ for myself. And she was right. I knew it as soon as I answered her question because I had not told her I had a real faith in God. I had tried to please him in my own way by becoming so much better as a person. God was still a stranger to me apart from the moments I spent in worship with others. Then I did feel some kind of closeness to him, but it never lasted. By Monday morning I was empty again and by Saturday night a total rebel. It was a full year after my first 'conversion' that God really came to me and entered into my life.

What led to my original 'conversion'? It was a willingness to believe because I knew that I needed it. That willingness was addressed by worship which I personally enjoyed for emotional and sensual reasons. I called it spiritual but in fact it was sensual. I enjoyed the music, the sense of tradition, the beauty of the building, the idea that I was involved in something sacred. It satisfied my emotional need for stability and purpose through reciting each week the same marvellous prayers and psalms. I felt close to God and responded accordingly with my willingness to conform. But I still did not know God.

That moment came when I was confronted with the state of my heart before him. I was proud before. Now I was proud of my religion. I was musical before. Now my music was religious. I was unbelieving before. Now I generous enough to offer my mind to God. When my sister asked if I knew Christ in my heart I was convicted of my own need. All the religious effort, all the changes I had proudly (and incompletely) made, were failed attempts to please God on my own terms. Nobody told me this. It was God's voice which I heard clearly for the first time. Until then I was not really sure that he even existed or whether I was still following an idea.

I argued with my sister all evening and missed going out to the pub with my friends! I defended myself, insulted her sincerity and assured her that I was as great a believer in Jesus as she was. But to no avail. By the end of the evening I was desperately certain I had not yet found the pardon and peace of Christ. I retreated to my room and prayed. I remember the words to this very day over thirty years later. 'God, I don't even know if you are there. But if you are and you will prove it to me you can have my life.'

Within a few days I was conscious of a change within me. I no longer wanted to live for myself but for God. I no longer had a emptiness of spirit within me but a definite fellowship with Jesus Christ which was constant throughout every waking moment. Some of the things which had bound me for years were suddenly broken in power, especially my foul mouth. For the first time in my life I was humbled in my heart in the presence of God.

What was the difference between my first and second 'conversion'? Essentially it was this. My first conversion was to the idea of Jesus and the pursuit of religion as 'a good thing for me'. I was moved, changed and to some extent satisfied by my experience but none of those things meant that Christ had become mine and I had become his. The religion I accepted was emotionally pleasing, reassuring and sensually delightful. All those things had become not helps but rather hindrances to finding the real thing.

The 'Conversion Experience'

You may think this story has nothing to do with postmodernism and modern evangelism because these have little to do with ancient prayers and classical music. But I will try to explain the relevance I see.

Firstly, my initial interest in Christianity was selfish. I was depressed about life, felt like a misfit with others, and held a philosophy which increased my despair. Christianity was a wonderful, though initially unbelievable, promise. I felt unloved, but God loved me. I was lonely and God would be my friend. My life was crumbling even as a thirteen-year-old and God would bring me peace and satisfaction. I was feeling bad about the excesses in my life and God could forgive my sins. I was converted to the benefits of being a Christian in the first instance.

Much of our evangelism today is based on this appeal. Come to Jesus in a meaningless world and have meaning. Come to Jesus with your unhappy experience of life and find a friend. Come to Jesus with your illnesses and burdens and he will cure you of them. But what about asking Jesus into your life? Surely, evangelicals are clear about this personal faith in a way my Anglican Church was sadly not. No. Just as I said prayers in the romantic gloom, modern evangelicals invite 'a prayer of decision' in the fervour and heat of 'feeling your need'. It is the same thing. Say a prayer and be blessed. Without God's work of conviction there is no real conversion.

Secondly, I found a church which pleased me emotionally and sensually by its style and worship. My taste was not everyone's to be sure. But it was my taste and the church I went to satisfied me. Music has always been a powerful mood changer for me and I came out of church 'feeling better' for having sung the ancient forms of music used there. I was affected by the reverence, the quiet, even the darkness of the church with its suggestion of God being in the shadows. There were so many shadows in my life and I had always seen them as fearful before then. In short, I was converted to an uplifting experience.

There is an increasing use of 'mood music' in evangelism and worship. We are excited by loud and professionally performed modern music. We are moved by romantic and quiet songs which never speak of the judgement of God but endlessly repeat assuring words of love. Even the lyrics have more to do with romantic experience than spiritual devotion – 'I love you, Jesus'. 'Your love is the meaning of my life' and so on. Words that could equally be sung about a girlfriend are sung about Jesus and God with about the same depth of meaning. We only have to mean it in the crisis of the moment and we can only mean it by becoming as emotional as possible in ourselves.

This kind of appeal to senses and emotion can, of course, be used by God and may sometimes be genuine. But the test of true love as we all know is less in saying some sentimental words and more in acting sacrificially and faithfully toward each other. The trouble with moods induced by atmosphere is that they are hugely unreal about the rest of the week. Many's 'converts' today are converts to the mood rather than the reality of loving God all week with their whole being.

This problem is made worse by the approach to evangelism which reduces conversion to a decision. I have just read Billy Graham's autobiography and I realize that he means something more by 'decision' than a mere set of words to ask Jesus into one's life. He was able to make that appeal in an age when most people still went to church but did not necessarily come to Christ. In the postmodern world the scene has changed. People do not know what they are deciding any more until they have sought after God seriously and learned the meaning of true conversion. Only then does the final decision represent a response to God rather than a response to emotional or personal need in life.

Conversion without God has become a real possibility. People today are lost in the deepest intellectual sense. There is no certainty left in a world of competing ideologies which are all wrong. There is no happiness left in a world of broken hearts and homes. There is no hope left in a world of uncertainty about tomorrow. Parents may separate, love may die, jobs may be 'downsized', careers may be lost. People move away from their families and roots, friendships cannot be trusted, rules are not obeyed. No authority is respected. That is the lostness of the postmodern age and Christianity has a powerful but misleading appeal when it comes with a bagful of earthly promises and a slick presentation using every gimmick of modern salesmanship and manipulation. People are so confused that any spirituality promises well, including the fleeting moment of well-being during a worship song at church.

The lostness of which the Bible speaks is spiritual, not emotional or physical. It embraces those other spheres but only because Jesus is Lord of everything, not because emotion equals spirituality or physical healing a spiritual salvation. It is sadly possible to come to God for all the benefits, and to enjoy the pleasures of good-feeling in church without ever knowing God. It is conversion without God.

That is not the end of the matter, however. Conversion without God is an experience of something less than God. What is it that people experience? There are two possibilities. We have already discussed the first: emotion, release of guilt, happiness – the experience of self. The second is an experience of another spiritual force which not only is less than God but also opposite to God.

Paul warns Timothy with these sobering words: '*the Spirit clearly says that in later times some will abandon the faith and follow deceiving spirits and things taught by demons. Such teachings come through hypocritical liars, whose consciences have been seared as with a hot iron*' (1 Tim. 4:1,2). Peter is just as certain that the demonic can enter into the story of Christian faith when he says '*Be self-controlled and alert. Your enemy the devil prowls around like a roaring lion looking for someone to devour*' (1 Pet. 5:8). Even the peaceable John who is so gentle in his writings says '*Dear friends, do not believe every spirit, but test the spirits to see whether they are from God, because many false prophets have gone out into the world*' (1 Jn. 4:1) These are warnings enough that within the Christian Church it is possible to be deceived not only about ourselves but also about the experience of dark spiritual powers whose master, according to 2 Corinthians 11:14, '*himself masquerades as an angel of light*' and who inspires '*false*

Christs and false prophets to appear and perform great signs and miracles to deceive even the elect – if that were possible.' (Mt. 24:24)

I have bothered to quote passages at this point because we need to see how universally the first Christians believed it was necessary to distinguish between God and the demonic within the very walls of the Christian Church. Modern evangelicals can be fascinated with demons while ignoring their potential to deceive people through an appearance of spirituality. Demons are far more likely to act in disguise than show their true colours. Deceit is the key word of the New Testament for describing them. Yet we imagine them only in crude medieval guise.

The most important passage of the New Testament regarding false conversion is Matthew chapter 13. It begins with the parable of the sower. There Jesus describes true and false conversion. The first false conversions is like the seed sown on the path which springs up only to die (v. 19). Then second is the seed sown on rocks which does not last (v. 20). Seed among thorns is the third, which is choked by the cares of life (v. 22). The good seed, the true conversion, is the one which brings fruit and lasts (v. 23). Having told this story, Jesus reinforces it with a story about weeds. They grow with the seed but are destined for burning (v. 40). Not all growth is to be accepted at face value in evangelism. That is a deeply sobering thought when evangelicalism has become as popular in society as it currently is.

Experience is the idol of the postmodern world. Religious experience can be engendered by atmosphere, auto-suggestion and even forms of mild hypnosis (which often benefit from mood and atmosphere in a meeting). Evangelicals must beware the temptation of making converts which God has not made, or the next generation of the church will be devastated by the consequences. We must resist the temptations offered by technology and music even though we may freely use these gifts of God to help us in genuine evangelism. The key is to keep the focus on the mind and the conscience. There are no true converts who are not first of all convicted of their spiritual rather than emotional or psychological need for God.

I remember reading a book on conversion by O. Hallesby. In it he tells the story of a boy who decided to help a butterfly escape from its chrysalis. Instead of letting the creature work itself free he peeled away the shell thinking to help it fly away. By doing so, the butterfly did not stretch its wings and was robbed of flight. That is what hasty counting of converts does. It tries to do God's work for him with disastrous results. There are more than a few people sitting in churches today who claim conversion but wonder why they have no appetite for God or true experience of him. They have never been given spiritual wings by the work of the Spirit.

Eight

Fellowship Without Relationships

Some years ago I met 'Colin'. He came to my church for six months before telling me he had become a Christian and wanted help to start living the Christian life. Colin attended a Beginner's Group and then a baptism class and eventually joined the church fellowship formally. He took an active part in church life, using his musical gifts in worship and becoming a much liked church member.

Two years later he turned up on the doorstep one night in tears of anger and frustration because his girlfriend of a year had jilted him. Until then I did not know he had a girlfriend because he had kept the relationship very quiet in the church. Then I discovered why she had ditched him. It was because she could not trust him to remain sober.

Why hadn't he shared his problem? Why had he kept his relationship from his friends? Why had the teaching we gave at the church about relationships and lifestyle had no effect? There was a simple explanation. Colin told me that he lived his life in compartments. At work he was the ultra-professional colleague who gave his best and expected it of others. He was not liked very much there, but he was widely respected as a worker. At church he was the active Christian who gave his gifts to the Lord and was pleased by the acceptance we offered him. At home on his own he was a drinker and lived a sometimes separate life from his church friends, going out to clubs and picking up girls with whom he developed sexual relationships. This time he had landed a lover who accepted his values – it was his business if on Sunday he was never around – but who disliked the constant drinking when they were together. Finally, the compartments broke down and he had to face bringing church and private life together on my doorstep.

Colin exemplifies a growing trend. People today increasingly live lives in separate boxes. Who they are at work is irrelevant to who they are at home. Who they are at home is not necessarily the same as when they are socializing. The reasons for this trend are complicated but very important.

Compartmentalized Living

First, in our mobile society people do not have a deep sense of identity built on family relations and roots in a community. People leave their home town and with it their grandparents, uncles, aunts and childhood friends. I always think of Paul Simon's song *My Little Town* as an excellent commentary on this phenomenon. One line goes, 'In my little town I grew up believing that God keeps his eye on us all'. That sense of being accountable was based on order and stability. It has all been lost in the mobile society. If you want to read a brilliant book about this, try *Future Shock* written by Alvin Tofler in the sixties. It was prophetic in its accuracy about this generation.

Second, we have lost any one agreed idea in Western life about the meaning of being alive. The Christian explanation is that we are made in the image of God and so are reasonable and moral human beings with an ideal to live up to. Our parents' generation rejected Christian values and went their own way. As a result we have no answer to the question 'Who am I?' Instead, we have grown up with the idea that we are sophisticated animals with no moral ideals except survival in 'the human jungle'.

Another factor is the television and computer age. Our self-awareness is not shaped by real relationships any more but rather by imaginary characters and scenes. As a result we live by making images of ourselves. In church we can be the spiritual seeker. At work we can be the ruthless salesman. At home we can be the magnificent lover or the kindly father or whatever it is we want out of our marriages and family circumstances. The different bits have no common thread except for the fact that we are there. We meet and relate to different people in each setting. It leads to a game which someone expressed as 'I'm OK, You're OK.' You accept me for what you see and I'll do the same. Whatever we do, we want to avoid having the image presented challenged, otherwise the whole edifice of who we are may crumble.

Added to these deep philosophical issues are some tragic practical facts. The greatest of these is the number of broken homes. When parents split up, the vast majority of fathers lose meaningful contact with their children after a few years. Even if this does not happen, children have to live with the knowledge that home life is unpredictable. They are not sure that they can count on their parents staying together and family life becomes a threatening rather than a wholesome and healing environment.

Another cause of instability and loss of deep relationships comes from being so mobile. A job may only last a few years in one town and so we cannot develop the kind of friendships which used to surround us when we lived in one place for many years. Not only that, we dare not form them because the wrench of losing them over and again becomes too painful to bear. Consequently, we retreat into greater privacy in life to protect ourselves.

The end result of these patterns and beliefs is that we are losing the art of keeping long and deep relationships in life. We relate to people on a 'temporary contract' which can expire at any moment because either we or the other person may move on – to other people or other places. We become defensive, private and inconsistent, waiting for something to go wrong rather than for something to get better.

That has led to an epidemic of loneliness in the postmodern age. Even in a crowd. We develop the survival skills of living within a private and isolated world and we lose the capacity to trust and take risks with our own security. We learn to wear images like badges which say 'this is who I am, accept me at face value'. It does not matter that tonight we wear one face and tomorrow another. That is part of our survival package in a hostile society.

The telly has long been our most constant companion and friend, the only one we can be sure will always be with us if we move or our families disintegrate. In the computer age that may well change. Today's children divide 'screen time' between the television and the computer game. As virtual-reality games develop over the next ten years, we will be able to construct imaginary friends and perhaps even sexual partners to play with. Real relationships are set to diminish even more.

Compartmentalized Christians

This process inevitably creeps into church life. We are conscientious Christians on Sunday morning, people who love our Bibles (now supplied by the church to save the embarrassment of loving it in the hostile public world). On Mondays we are the all-efficient workers who give everything to the job. On Saturday night we are the fun-loving group member out for a good time. No one can challenge the game because all are playing along.

But the problem goes deeper than that. How often have you played the church game of 'How are you – fine – so am I – God bless you?' It used to be a symptom of the British stiff upper lip but things have moved on since then. Now it is a symptom of rejecting any intrusion by the church into our private lives. The consequences are enormous.

Moral discipline is collapsing among Christian young people. I have for years attended a major Christian holiday week. I have noticed an increasing tendency for young people to go there not for the meetings but for the opportunity to 'party' under the nose of the Christian programme. In the local church, the same young people separate their private lives from their church ones. Gone is the discipline of making relationships primarily within the church in favour of joining a group of school-friends for social activities. Even more precarious is the old (and biblical) rule that Christians should only date fellow Christians. The number of 'divided marriages' is increasing as women especially look for partners outside the family of faith. It is a sad fact, the difficult consequences of which are seldom faced until it is too late. Private life is becoming a 'no-go' area for the Christian Church regarding its own members.

Another consequence is the wooden way in which people relate to each other in church. We are called to love one another but in order to keep up that pretence we have to change the meaning of love. It is no longer the deep commitment of friendship and mutual care but the sugar-sweet experience of temporary *bonhomie* sealed with a loving hug during communion. Hospitality becomes extremely selective and social events fail because people are too busy with their private lives to allow more time than Sunday morning to the church.

We still talk about 'belonging to a church' but we have reversed the meaning. The church belongs to us in the sense that when we want it, it should be there; and when we don't, nobody should mind. Regular attendance means 'now and again' and at the best 'once a week'. What a far cry from the days when on Sundays we went for teaching in the morning, all-age Sunday School in the afternoon, evangelistic events in the evening, Prayer Meeting on Monday, Bible Study on yet another evening of the week and then other programmes in addition. In such an environment love meant deep relationships and sustained fellowship. What real love can flourish when people see each other infrequently and only exchange a few bland and hurried sentences when they do? Yet that is the modern church.

The consumer society has invaded the church. We go to take what we want from it rather than give what it needs, either in money or personal involvement. Highly capable people withhold their gifts from the church on the basis of the pressures they face through home and work. Even when they do offer to serve, their criterion for working is not that it fulfils the church's mission but that it fulfils the person's desire for achievement or desire to serve. Wealthier people will even give more money so that someone else can do the work they would have done themselves in a previous generation. That is one of the reasons that staff appointments are growing in middle-class churches. It is not a sign of progress in mission but of failure in fellowship.

Yet another result of postmodern loneliness in the church is the growth of pastoral problems. When people were depressed or lonely in church years ago they would have a network of friends among whom were strong and committed Christians who could share their burdens. Now the best they have is a fortnightly or weekly housegroup where the talk is public and therefore exposed. Who are they to turn to in need? The professionals. The minister must now be a counsellor as well as a pastor. He must have the ability not only to guide people through the Bible and spiritual living, but through deep psychological problems. Ministers meanwhile are less respected for their spiritual and theological gifts and are judged increasingly on the basis of whether they are 'helpful', 'kindly', and so on.

The result is that we spend less and less time on teaching the church and more and more on healing broken lives and hearts. Once we were shepherds of the flock. Now we are becoming sheepdogs who must incessantly round up an ever-increasing number of strays. The work of the ministry is becoming that of a psychologist.

Yet another effect of the postmodern taste for shallowness in church is that congregational worship is becoming shallow with it. Merely worshipping God is no longer adequate. Worship must be fast moving, entertaining and above all full of the 'feel-good factor'. Sermons on sin are out. Sermons on service are out. Sermons are out, replaced by the stand-up comic routine which brings a smile of pleasure to a tired and listless people. The shallow church follows, a church where 'evangelical' means 'experience centred', and good experience at that.

All these things are consequences of the postmodern loss of self-identity and meaningful relationships. Life is no longer allowed to be serious. We go to church to be entertained and consoled, to be uplifted and blessed, but not to give ourselves to God and each other in love. The irony is that as the world goes further and further down this road life does not get less serious and painful but more so. Unhappiness becomes a plague when people do not relate to each other. We become empty of human meaning because that meaning is primarily found in deep personal relationships. The number of young people, especially men, who commit suicide has grown in the same period that relationships have broken down. The face of homelessness has changed for the same reason. Once, a walk down London's Embankment would reveal a collection of traditional tramps accompanied by hopeless alcoholics. Now the usual sight is of young men and women who have left the security of their homes because they cannot relate any more to their families.

The Christian Church should be the alternative society. It should be the place where the broken-hearted find healing, where friendships are deepest of all, where love is a meaningful word. Instead, the church has become like the world. We pray for revival but long before revival can come the evangelical church must rediscover her biblical foundations and drive a wedge between herself and the world in which she now languishes.

Of course, the scene is not all bad. There are loving churches and there are faithful churches. Unfortunately, they are too often different churches! The secret of recovery is to bring together loving life in the Spirit and strong biblical ministry. Conservative evangelicals need to realize just how deadening their world can easily become with its fear of immediacy with God and other people. Charismatics need to realize that endless spiritual 'love-ins' sustained by storytelling preachers – or harangues on loyalty – cannot replace deep, scholarly, searching and relevant doctrinal Christianity.

The answer to our lostness in the modern world is not to make the church more and more like the world but less and less like it in spiritual values. It may be necessary to dethrone the god of numerical success in evangelical life and return to the worship of a God who is allowed to make serious demands on his followers. Otherwise, the evangelical church may fulfil Neil Postman's description of modern society as 'entertaining ourselves to death'.

Nine

Spirituality Without Selflessness

New Age Spirituality

The New Age of postmodernism is concerned with spirituality in a big way. The variety of spiritual movements is immense, from Eastern mysticism to ancient witchcraft with every conceivable alternative in between. This fascination with 'being spiritual' is one of the great surprises of the modern age, following as it does the attempt to reduce human existence to the status of being nothing more than an intelligent animal. Despite our new interest in the Western world, however, selfishness has also grown apace so that people want a spirituality which is essentially painless. There are three main reasons why.

First, the earlier decades of this century were hard and sacrificial ones. Families sacrificed their teenage sons in the First World War on a dreadful scale all too easily forgotten today. Then came years of financial hardship between the World Wars, when our grandparents struggled to obtain the basic necessities of life. More austerity followed with another World War, making our nations determined to achieve lasting stability and prosperity.

Second, the spiritual and moral foundations of Western life have been systematically eroded by materialism. People live for physical and material well-being today. The new emphasis on being spiritual is not an alternative to but an aspect of having everything this life can offer.

Third, the spiritual vacuum left by materialism has been filled by the pursuit of self. This pursuit has largely taken the form of seeking self-understanding and fulfilment. The self *is* the spiritual dimension as far as most people are now concerned. At the same time the eighties produced a view of life in which community values were dismissed. Margaret Thatcher famously declared that 'there is no such thing as society'. Her words were symptomatic of a fundamental shift in which the pursuit of self has altered from being morally dubious to being morally worthy. The idea of self-denial has almost come to be seen as harmful.

Self-fulfilment in the New Age is an aspect of spirituality. People are spiritual if they not only live 'animal' lives but 'self-aware' ones too. Secular science proclaimed 'man' to be an intelligent ape whose morality was determined strictly in terms of evolution and animal behaviour. The explanation of human life was that we evolved intelligence more successfully than other species and evolved a moral system based on that success. We protect human life, therefore, not as an absolute moral virtue but as a means of ensuring the human race remains strong.

The New Age of postmodernism has rejected this stark and inadequate explanation of existence because we actually do experience life as something more. In particular, we have rediscovered another dimension to it which evolutionists and secular scientists neither explained nor seemed to care about. There is, to use a famous phrase, 'a ghost in the machine' of the human mind and body.

But it often goes no further than a belief in ghosts! The spirituality of the postmodern age is the pursuit of that ghost in order to be at peace with it. Every experience of self, whether derived from a meditation or a counselling session is seen as fulfilling our spiritual need. This preoccupation with the ghostly self has crept into evangelical life in a number of ways.

The 'Feel-Good Factor'

To begin with, evangelical experience is increasingly seen in selfish terms. Personal spiritual experience has become monotonously upbeat. Gone is the emphasis on repentance and humility before God. Gone is the sense of entering the holiest place with God. In their place we have 'blessing'. And what is this blessing? Feeling good about God and with God.

The one experience of God which is sure to be welcomed is that of his loving acceptance and care. Songs about loving God and being loved by him are reduced to expressions of emotion. It is more a case of 'being in love' with God – or more accurately just feeling it for the moment.

The Fatherhood of God in the Bible is first of all a statement about his relationship with Jesus Christ his Son. It expresses the sovereignty of the Father over the Son and the Spirit as well as the love they share with each other. But the modern evangelical church is not interested in the control of God the Father. Sovereignty conflicts with our freedom to do as we like. Consequently, God the Father has become God the sugar-daddy who indulges us by answering our every prayer with approval and blessing.

The Fatherhood of God in the Bible is conditional. It is a relationship he gives exclusively to his Son for all eternity. To Christ, the Father is unconditionally committed and accepting. His every prayer is answered, his every approach is accepted, his every heartbeat is precious to the Father – and vice versa. The Son is totally committed to the Father in submission and obedience, a fact measured in human history by his lowly birth, his sinless life and his amazing submission even to death upon the cross.

This relationship with the Father is extended in its totality to those who are 'in Christ'. The Christian experiences the love of God as Father, to be sure. But the true Christian has also the same attitude as Christ toward the Father, including submission and even obedience 'unto death'. That kind of relationship has been obscured to the point of denial in a world where blessing is not closeness to God as Father but mere acceptance of goodies from 'Dad'.

Spiritual Power

Spiritual strength is further defined as spiritual power in the same way as it is defined in New Age understanding, which views spirituality as a power over circumstances, for self-fulfilment and happiness. A New Age spiritualist is someone who, though not able to find peace and happiness, 'knows a man who can' – or more accurately, a force which is willing to be of apparent service. The wiccan can control the forces of nature. The psychic healer can mysteriously conquer illnesses. The carrier of spiritual stones can ward off evil and be attuned to 'positive forces'. In some circles it is even believed that human life can become in some way divine, as the actress Shirley MacLaine has boldly claimed for herself.

These attitudes have been mirrored exactly within the evangelical world, especially among some charismatics. At the most extreme end we have heard the heresy that Christians share divinity with Jesus. The 'health and wealth' movement claims unlimited spiritual authority over life. But even among more mainstream Christians spirituality has come to equal spiritual authority over life shared with God. It is common to hear people pray, 'We give you permission, Lord'. This is dangerously close to confusing human co-operation with control over God. Illness or hardship is increasingly seen as always evil and therefore something to be banished with enough prayer and faith.

The prayer team has emerged in church life but frequently it is not so much an intercessory ministry for people as a power ministry to people, as though praying for someone transfers power from the prayer partner to the one prayed for. We need to encourage much more prayer, of course, and prayer teams can be a great blessing to people in need. But there is a vast difference between intercessors bringing the needy to Jesus and bringing them to themselves instead.

The emphasis on power has led to a very unbalanced and partial view of spiritual gifts. Gifts which suggest spiritual privilege with God become the major ones, especially speaking in tongues and prophecy. Gifts which suggest humble or loyal service, like giving money, providing hospitality, or even Bible teaching become second class. This is despite the clear primacy given to teaching in the New Testament and despite the lowliness of tongue speaking recorded with equal clarity.

Spirituality is also defined as material success. Blessing today increasingly is measured by financial security and good circumstances. The idea that God might bless someone with hardship and trial does not figure in this materialistic outlook, making the Lord Jesus Christ's life of service in poverty and sacrifice a very model of failure! I feel I have to plead here against being misunderstood. It is true that blessing includes material and physical well-being and it is true that God supplies all our needs. What is not true is that we are allowed to define our needs over against God's will. What is not true is that all wealth and health are blessings and all illness and hardship are not.

Finally, spirituality is defined as private rather than corporate. This is where the individualist and self-centred world of the eighties wrecks church life. We do not go to church in order to walk together through life but to share together through an hour or two. Corporate blessing is what happens experientially to 'me' and a lot of other people in the same 'me centred' way. The life of the church may then extend no further than the period we spend in worship together. Relationships of love, works of mercy, evangelism in teams, practical tasks in the church's life – all these things have become optional extras in the Christian life which bear no relationship to the claimed spirituality or consecration of the Christian. As long as we are 'blessed' we are strong and fulfilling the Christian calling. The purpose of the church is no longer then to call me into service but to buoy me up for the week to come.

The Bible's Answer

What is wrong with this Christianity? Largely it is that Christians have become dualists about the power of God and Satan. All 'bad' things come from the devil who is in opposition to God and may rob us of his blessing. Gone is the idea that Satan is bound, that he serves the purpose of God despite himself, that he is essentially weak before the truth and authority of Jesus Christ so that his attempts to destroy God's plan and purpose have been taken captive by the risen Christ.

The very people who proclaim their victory over him give him too much credit for everything that appears to go wrong. Where is the God who in all things '*works for the good of those who love him, who have been called according to his purpose*' (Rom. 8:28)? Evangelicals are increasingly allowing themselves to live in as haunted a universe as the spiritualists of the New Age, and often use the same techniques to address it. Blessing 'falls' through mind alteration techniques more familiar to stage hypnotists. God's answer is delivered through prayers that come perilously close to spell casting done in the name of Jesus.

Along with our capitulation to the spirit of the age (or should it be the Spirit of This Age?) such evangelicals have lost sight of their own spiritual tradition derived from the principles of Scripture.

Go back to the great spiritual giants of the Reformation and the Puritans and you will find a very different view of the matter. Spirituality concerned knowing God through 'the means of grace'. Those means were both private and public.

In private we were taught to walk with God through bringing the whole of our lives into fellowship with him in prayer and biblical obedience for all matters of faith and life. Conscious fellowship with God was not a matter of God showing himself in exceptional circumstances but showing himself in Christ throughout all the ordinary things of life. A walk with God meant going through the daily routine of life conscious at each turn of being united with Christ by faith and consecrated to Christ by obedience. There were no areas where self was honoured; indeed self-preoccupation was the opposite of Christ's lordship over life.

The 'public means of grace' concerned life in the church: receiving the Word, giving faithful worship together, exercising spiritual gifts for the good of all and obeying Christ in baptism and the Lord's Supper. These things fed faith and brought the

Christian into fellowship with other Christians so that Christ manifested himself among us. There was no possibility of life with Christ apart from real relationships within the fellowship of the church. The church was central to spiritual life, not just as the source of blessings when the worship went well but as the constant source of Christ's presence guaranteed by the very promise of Jesus himself. To serve the church was to serve the Lord. To love the church was to love the Lord. To be in church was to be in the presence of Christ in the most special and certain way. This church focus has been all but abandoned in the postmodern age of individualism.

Another vital component of spirituality was to conform our character to the character of Christ. His life was no model of failure, no exception to the modern rule, but rather the most sublime and certain manifestation of true spirituality. It was not that people modelled themselves on his physical life (as in the monastic movement) but that people modelled themselves on his relationship with God as a man: his prayer life, his dealings with others, his self-understanding as a servant and son of God in the flesh. Bad theology and doctrine have obscured the distinctions we need to make here. We have maintained the divinity of Christ as Son of God but not nearly enough his perfect humanity as Son of Man. Imitate his divine sonship and you make yourself into another Christ. Imitate his human sonship and you sanctify your life with God as he did on earth. The old word for this was 'godliness'. It is a constant theme of the Old and New Testament teaching about walking with God.

One more element in biblical spirituality deserves mention. Life with God meant life for God. The whole of life was meant to be lived in conscious obedience to God's revealed will in Scripture. There are biblical principles for a godly home, a godly nation, recreation, sex, church order – you name it and Scripture addresses it. The way of godliness was the way of walking in God's ways made known in Scripture. No word of prophecy could alter it, no blessing circumvent it, no preacher contradict it.

This is the area where evangelicals have most lost touch with biblical authority. We have reduced walking with God to being filled with the Spirit. Once filled (supposedly) we then 'walk in the Spirit' by which is too often meant listening to our feelings as the vehicle of God's voice. This is a cheap short cut to God's blessing on our lives, where we give up reading and learning the principles and deep truths of Scripture so that we hear the Word of God in our hearts because we rely on 'feeling led of the Spirit'. It is a shame upon us and a scandal in a world which is more than ever in need of hearing the true Word of God through his people.

Part Three

The Church God Wants

Ten

A Church of the Book

When I became a Christian at the age of fourteen my converted
friends took me to a bookshop and helped me choose a Bible.
They told me the most important single step I could take in my
spiritual life was to begin reading and studying God's Word
because God would speak to me through its pages and direct my
Christian life. In many evangelical churches today the first thing
a new Christian is told is to sign up for next year's Bible Week.
The place of the Bible has been altered in evangelicalism from
being the primary source of spiritual inspiration to being an
optional extra in the evangelical world.

There are several reasons for this change. One of the most
significant is undoubtedly the emergence of the charismatic renewal with its emphasis on personal guidance from the Holy
Spirit. Why read the Bible for guidance when you can receive a
message from God just for you? Another reason is the decline in
biblical preaching. The average evangelical preacher is boring,
irrelevant and lacking in biblical content. It is no wonder that
people do not value preaching any more when it is so badly done
in many of our evangelical churches.

Even when the preaching is biblically based it is still done in a
way which does not connect with the real world. The truths of
the Bible are too often locked up in an academic presentation of
doctrines the end result of which is nothing more than being 'well
taught'. The Puritans preached their society into a political revolution. Whatever you may think of that episode in British history,
the evangelical church was at the centre of life privately and

publicly. There is no danger of that now. Even the charismatic renewal, for all its use of modern style, is a world away from radically challenging the society in which we now live. Indeed, the opposite is true. The church is so like the world in its appeal and style that professionalism rather than godliness is the order of the day. In order to win a new generation, the evangelical church needs to go back to its own foundations for faith.

The Authority of Scripture

The Bible is the inspired truth revealed by God. This claim is made in various ways within the pages of Scripture. In the Old Testament Scripture is the final judge of truth: *'To the law and to the testimony! If they do not speak according to this word, they have no light of dawn'* (Isa. 8:20). The truthfulness and trustworthiness of Scripture is summed up in the famous verse from Psalm 119:105: *'Your word is a lamp to my feet and a light to my path.'* Jesus portrayed the same absolute allegiance to Scripture in his statement *'man does not live on bread alone, but on every word that comes from the mouth of God'* (Mt. 4:4). The centrality of Scripture to the Christian life is demonstrated in his prayer for the future church just hours before his final ordeal and execution when he prayed, *'sanctify them by the truth; your word is truth'* (Jn. 17:17).

The authority of Scripture has come under a great deal of criticism from inside as well as outside the Christian Church. It has been argued that Scripture is a human product even if it is inspired by God and therefore we have to make differences between parts which are inspired and parts which are not. The relationship between human and divine authorship is actually described, however, in the New Testament. In 2 Peter 1:20 we are told, *'Above all, you must understand that no prophecy of Scripture came about by the prophet's own interpretation. For prophecy never had its origin in the will of man, but men spoke from God as they were carried along by the Holy Spirit.'* Scripture is *'God-breathed'* (2 Tim. 3:16). It comes from the mouth of God with a divine authority which is not overruled or lost by its human authorship. It is fully divine in authority yet fully human in authorship. There are differences of style and culture among its authors. They have particular concerns and interests, even within the first three gospels which use much of the same material. '*Men spoke*' – of that there can be no doubt and the study of those human elements is no threat to biblical authority. Yet for all those differences, '*men spoke from God*'. That is what makes Scripture authoritative and calls every disciple of Christ to say with him that we live by every word it contains.

These and many other biblical passages leave us in no doubt that Scripture claims divine authority in its entirety. But we have not yet grasped the real nature of that authority. It is not just that God has spoken and Scripture is the result, but rather that God has spoken and has never stopped speaking through his revelation in Scripture. It is a living word, not a dead letter. So the writer of Hebrews says of Scripture, '*For the word of God is living and active. Sharper than any double-edged sword, it penetrates even to dividing soul and spirit, joints and marrow; it judges the thoughts and attitudes of the heart*' (Heb. 4:12). A similar thought occurs in 1 Peter 1:23: '*For you have been born again, not of perishable seed, but of imperishable, through the living and abiding word of God.*' The authority of Scripture is not defined by merely asserting its accuracy, something evangelicals have focused on rather exclusively. The reason Scripture is binding is that it contains and communicates the presence and reality of the living God. God speaks through his living Word. To receive the Scriptures is a spiritual experience before it is an intellectual task. There is a dynamic authority to Scripture which is as present now to the modern reader as if God spoke the words to us from heaven for the first time. To read Scripture is a spiritual experience and not merely an intellectual pursuit. It is not only a helpful spiritual experience but an essential one for every true believer. For it is by this means that Christ prayed we would be sanctified and grow closer to God. There is no walk with God except one founded upon the devoted reading and obeying of his Word. How have evangelicals lost this emphasis on Scripture? In two ways – a conservative evangelical way and a charismatic way.

The conservative evangelical mistake is to become over-intellectual about the Bible. It has become a book from which doctrines are to be extracted, a book to be defended against liberal humanist attacks, a book to be revered for teaching truth. The evangelical boast is 'I believe the Bible.' But we may believe things which are irrelevant to us in practice. I believe in Africa but I have never been there and have no great burden to go. Believing in something does not establish a relationship, but rather an attitude. It might be better for us to stop talking so much about believing the Bible as the supreme act of allegiance and to speak rather of receiving it. To receive the Bible is to accept its authority whether I understand it or not, whereas merely to believe the Bible is to stamp the authority of our approval upon it as if we had grasped it all and come to a decision. To receive the Bible as God's Word is to involve the emotions and will, whereas simply to believe the Bible is to leave it all in the realm of the intellect – the Enlightenment touch on evangelicalism once again.

The charismatic fault with regard to the Bible comes from a wrong understanding of prophecy and similar spiritual gifts. There is a strand of teaching which places 'revelation now' on a level with biblical revelation. The Bible was God's Word then, and this prophecy is God's Word now.

The claim is a false one. Prophecy today does have that human element which may confuse or obscure the divine Word. That is why prophecy must be tested (1 Cor. 14:29). Furthermore, there are no new truths to be revealed since Christ is the final revelation (Heb. 1:1ff). Even the New Testament letters do not add new truths to Christ but expound the teaching of the Old Testament in the light of Christ. So Paul preaches justification by faith and not by the works of the law. So the writer of Hebrews draws wonderful spiritual lessons from the worship and ceremonies of the Temple. They do not bring additional light to that of Christ but rather focus the rays of his light on the different situations and concerns of the New Testament Church. Revelation has ceased having reached its fullness in Jesus Christ.

Failure to grasp the relationship between Christ and Scripture has led evangelicalism into a position in which it is ill-equipped to address the postmodern world. It is assumed that the postmodern age will not tolerate 'old-fashioned' biblical teaching because we are now experience based. According to this logic we should tell stories rather than explain and expound the Bible. Instead of preaching the biblical model of conversion we should present Jesus in modern terms, perhaps as a kind of counsellor and support in the lostness of the postmodern world.

In fact, Scripture is the key to addressing the postmodern age. Scripture is experiential in authority. It speaks to the human condition precisely because it is the living and abiding Word of God. A preacher may miss his mark. A conversation may lose its thread. A story may fail to convey the gospel message. People may turn to Christ as a counsellor and helper but not for the forgiveness of sin and reconciliation with God. But the Word of God is a living seed which brings forth spiritual fruit when it is boldly proclaimed to people. We do not have to argue for its truthfulness because it carries its own persuasiveness within.

The heart of biblical authority has been lost. The intellectual approach makes the Bible into a textbook of facts. How do we know it is 'true'? Because it is internally consistent, because its prophecies have been fulfilled, because it records facts, some of which have been proved as such after considerable doubt. This is all very well, but people may grow up with no doubt that the Bible is all these things and with an expert knowledge of its contents; yet they may not encounter God despite their knowledge. Something is lacking unless God opens the eyes of the reader to his presence in Scripture. Calvin, the great French Reformer, called this 'the internal testimony of the Holy Spirit'.

Experience-based Christians might seem at first to be nearer the truth about the Bible because they emphasize personal experience which resembles the experience of the people in the Bible. But really it is only a variation on the same theme. Where more mind-focused people look for ideas which can be confirmed today, this approach looks for experiences which can be confirmed today. They look for different things but in the same way – for things by which to prove the Bible to be true.

In fact, nothing can 'prove' the Bible to be true except the witness of God's Holy Spirit. It is as we receive the Word of God by reading it with faith in Christ that its living power grips our lives and calls us to belief. The place of the Bible in the Christian life is not determined by permission either of the intellectual or of the charismatically powerful person. It is determined by the fact that from the very beginning God spoke to a community who are the people of God and his speaking is enshrined in Scripture. God spoke and still speaks through this Word.

The Centrality of Scripture

Both the conservative evangelical and the charismatic need to go back to the centrality of Scripture in the Christian's experience. The evangelical experience is largely presented as conversion, the charismatic experience as baptism in the Spirit. The biblical experience is a lifelong dialogue with God, hearing him in Scripture and speaking to him in the heart. If we are to go back to the Scriptures as the living Word of God then we must make it central again to evangelical faith and life.

First, it must be central in worship. In worship we approach God and he approaches us. This fact is promised by Christ who said that *'where two or three come together in my name, there am I with them'*. But how does God make himself known? By his self-revelation in Scripture. Experience-centred worship takes the emphasis away from Scripture to the inner self. How do I feel? Did I receive a blessing? These are not the questions of spiritual reality but of emotional intensity. Conversely, if I have grappled with the teaching of Scripture I have heard God speak to me. If I have sought to bring my life into submission to the Word proclaimed I have sought to draw close to God. It is out of that encounter with Scriptural truth that an encounter with God occurs.

If Scripture is central to worship, the reading of Scripture is a central act in worship. This is a point at which both conservatives and charismatics fall down badly. I have been to charismatic acts of worship where the Bible is not read at all, or if it is the reading has been a very minor and badly done event. People rush through it, failing to give it proper reverence and careful emphasis. In more conservative churches the Bible reading may be no more carefully done and may be unconnected to the sermon which should expound it.

Scripture must be made central again in our personal lives. The place where God deals with his children is in the heart informed by God's truth. Prayer must not be a dialogue between my emotions and myself but between God and myself. It is not a 'feeling' which communicates God to the soul but the Word of God encountered. That truth is a lamp and a light to our lives, as the Psalmist says. We live godly lives when we live in its light.

The primary way in which God speaks to us is through Scripture, and not simply through the words of Scripture but through its principles for life, its practical examples of godly living and its teachings about a true relationship with God. It is only when we have become steeped in its message that we can judge rightly the personal guidance of the Holy Spirit. He never speaks differently from Scripture and he seldom speaks apart from it. Even when we 'are led' by the Spirit into a course of action the leading is more certain when it is reinforced by a biblical principle or example of action.

Perhaps the gravest omission in modern evangelicalism is the disregard we pay to the relation between the Bible and our public world of society and culture. The Bible addresses standards of behaviour in the workplace and the home. The Bible contains many instructions about the good government of society. Even questions of art and music are dealt with in the pages of the Word of God, inspiring the Christian to approve of everything that is true and beautiful in life. Because we have neglected this aspect of biblical teaching, the cutting edge of the evangelical faith has been all but lost among believers. Evangelicalism is no longer a challenge to the unbelieving world but a chameleon within it, changing colour with every cultural trend so as to remain on friendly terms with the surrounding world. The revolutionary power of the gospel has been abandoned for a lack of biblical instruction and obedience.

It is time for evangelicals to return to the Scriptures and believe that within it is contained the way of life and truth for ourselves and the world in which we live. There is a spiritual vacuum in the postmodern world which cries out to be filled with authentic Christian faith. If we fail in this endeavour we must not be surprised when some other ideology or religion takes the place of Christianity as the driving force of the next generation. Never has the opportunity been greater since the Reformation itself.

Eleven

A Spiritual Church

Over the last ten years of my ministry I have accumulated a vast number of adverts for leadership conferences. Some of them are about evangelism. Some of them are about being Spirit-filled and powerful in accordance with some leader or church or new movement. Most of them are about becoming more professional in church leadership, creating better worship, better structures, better techniques. This is the hope of the evangelical world for the next millennium.

When I look back over the same period in my ministry and think about the conversions which have lasted I form a different picture of success. I think of a New Age hippy who was converted when she attended a Christmas service. Her life was transformed from real degradation to reflect the love of Christ. Then there was a demon-possessed young man in a homosexual relationship whose life has changed completely by the power of God. Another woman I think of was lost in a world of spiritual searching without finding until she met with Christ. Yet another convert was in her seventies who told me that finding Christ was the end of a search for spiritual reality which had begun with childhood attendance at church.

The Secret of Lasting Success

I could multiply the examples but the connecting thread between them all is that they met with Jesus Christ in quite ordinary services. I conclude from this that the evangelical church already has the message and the means it needs for confronting the postmodern age. The secret of our success is not in some new technique or system for evangelism and church management but in the passionate proclamation of Jesus Christ as Saviour and Lord. Sometimes we evangelicals cannot see the wood for the trees in all our hyped-up marketing of new ideas. However, I am bound to say that having the message is not enough in itself. My own experience in the ministry demonstrated something to me which I believe is the missing element in much of our church life.

I was converted at the age of fourteen and discipled in my faith through strong Bible teaching and an emphasis on serious commitment. When God called me into ministry I went through university and theological college and was ordained at the age of twenty-two. By that time I had developed my approach to ministry on the basis that the Bible was the inspired truth from God which, when preached, would be powerful and effective. Did not Paul say '*I am not ashamed of the gospel, because it is the power of God for the salvation of everyone who believes*' (Rom. 1:16)?

I went to a small village church in the Black Mountains of South Wales and duly started to proclaim this gospel fearlessly and passionately. One young person was converted in the first few weeks but then went away to university. For six months I continued to labour with no further result. What was wrong? Why didn't the gospel have the effect I longed for and believed in?

I began to meet and pray with a fellow minister each week. We would spend every Monday morning in worship together. One morning, something happened to us which changed my life and my ministry. Every attempt to describe it fails to convey its solemn power in my life. God came down upon us and we were bathed in his presence for hours which passed like minutes. We were unable to speak, we were unable even to open our eyes in case we saw the glory of God.

At some point during that morning God spoke to me unmistakably about my work for him and promised me spiritual fruit. I had entered that room humiliated and desperate. I left it with total confidence in God's calling and purpose for my life.

Conversions began to flow in my ministry and I live to this day with the anointing I was given. I have not always valued it or used it. I have sometimes contradicted it in my life and seen it ebb as well as flow. But it is there by a divine commission I dare not ever deny. That experience taught me several lessons about biblical authority.

First, it is not enough merely to accept the Bible for its truth. Unless the Holy Spirit anoints its use our proclamation remains a dead letter: for God *'has made us competent as ministers of a new covenant – not of the letter but of the Spirit; for the letter kills, but the Spirit gives life'* (2 Cor. 3:6). I began to read about the lives of the early evangelical leaders and I found that such experiences were not only common among them but essential to their ministries. They were not simply men (and women) of the book but of the Spirit as well.

Second, I learned that I do not have to be a perfect Christian in order to be a useful one. There were still sins in my life with which I battled – and still do. I am still capable of behaving in ways which are less than Christlike. I learned that God uses imperfect people for his kingdom purposes. You only have to read the New Testament to see that this is true. Paul was occasionally blunt and unyielding. Peter notoriously failed to live up to his convictions about Gentiles coming to faith and had a massive showdown with Paul over it. Timothy had to be encouraged to avoid timidity in leadership. Demas went off the tracks. Yet God anointed these imperfect people and he still does. Hallelujah!

Seeking God's Empowering

Evangelicalism has not always remembered its early history regarding the empowering of the Holy Spirit. At the beginning of the twentieth century, however, the Pentecostal movement began a new trend with its remarkable story of growth into what is now the largest evangelical movement in existence. More conservative evangelicals may not agree with its distinctive belief that the New Testament supernatural gifts had been restored, but one thing is certainly true: the Pentecostal and charismatic tradition has put power for mission back on the evangelical agenda.

There is much to be said in praise of the world-wide charismatic renewal in terms of evangelism, fellowship and the desire to serve God's kingdom purposes with total zeal and abandonment. The certainty given by baptism in the Spirit that God is personally at work in your life and is equipping you to serve him is part of the genius and explanation of charismatic growth. When God is for you, who can be against you?

However, the older evangelical emphasis on conversion as the great experience deserves greater attention. The trouble is that whereas the early evangelicals made conversion a solemn and momentous event which was indeed a baptism in the Spirit, modern evangelicals have often made it a cheap decision to 'accept Christ'. This version of conversion is frequently nothing more than a mild emotional choice between being accepted or rejected by God. It has robbed the evangelical mainstream of any real experiential dimension. What follows such decisions is inevitably the need for something more because the original is so shallow. It is part of the appeal of charismatic life that the believer is offered that 'something more'.

There are two realities which evangelicalism must face about its lack of emphasis on conversion. The first is that the process has been made so shallow it can easily be imitated or mistaken. Unless we return to preaching the staggering cost of salvation in the cross and the radical meaning of discipleship we cannot win this battle.

The second is that there *is* something more, experientially, than a mild and cheap conversion to Jesus! The New Testament is full of the works of God in the lives of believers and in the life of the church. People were not converted only to a life of faithful obedience and devotion but to a life constantly renewed and changed by the Holy Spirit. Evangelicalism has a bad habit of restricting that dimension to past revivals.

The challenge to evangelicalism is to seek after God's empowering until we receive it. We have bottled this issue up in an argument over words. One person says the baptism of the Spirit occurs at conversion and then the Christian has all there is of God.

Another says that there is a second experience of baptism in the Spirit. Another says there is a second experience but it is of filling not baptism. What surely matters is that there is such a thing as the experience of God the Holy Spirit empowering and gifting the Christian Church for its mission. I remember vividly George Verwer speaking at Bristol University when I was an undergraduate there. He said of the empowering of the Holy Spirit, 'I don't care what you call it; get it!' That is the crying need of the evangelical church.

The great mistake which charismatics make with the Holy Spirit is the selfish context in which he is so often sought and offered. He is presented as something essentially personal to the believer, something to help the Christian life along, something to bolster up weak and inadequate faith and failed Christian living, something to bless our Christianity rather than to lead us into mission. Very often the emphasis is on an emotional experience for personal satisfaction. That is not the message of the New Testament, which portrays Pentecost not as a spiritual convention but as a missionary commissioning service!

The conservative evangelical church needs to wake up and realize that a clinical service containing an intellectual message will not address our postmodern society in which people are starving for reality in their lives. The church must become a community in which God is felt and seen at work. True spiritual experience matters and if that is absent from a church that church would do well to abandon every programme except those for prayer and evangelism. Pray the blessing down, then preach it out! If we believe the Bible, what right do we have to lock it up in our subcultures of dead escapism and dreary worship?

The charismatic world needs to understand that life without truth is as wrong as truth without life. If we believe the Bible enough to seek the same kind of church it portrays, we should believe it enough to follow the same kind of doctrine it teaches. The Bible is no more a textbook of ideas for worship than it is a merely a textbook of doctrine. It is the living Word which is used by the Holy Spirit in its entirety to bring life to the believer and to the waiting world.

The great issue at stake here is how to test the reality of the Holy Spirit. The evangelical mistake is to avoid the emotions, but the charismatic one is to identify them with God. A person 'feels led' because he or she 'feels'. Not every feeling is God-inspired. The Holy Spirit does not work through either the mind or the emotions but through the whole inner person, the soul. That will involve, in perfect balance, the mind, heart and will.

Mind and Heart and Will

The way forward for the whole evangelical world is to restore the biblical place of these three faculties together as expressions of the soul. God works in the soul and convicts of truth in the mind, gives experience of the truth in the emotions and gives desire for obedience in the will. Will-Christianity alone is slavish obedience. Mind-Christianity alone is an intellectual game. Heart-Christianity alone is an emotional trip. God does not enter into a person's life through these things as if they were gates, but rather manifests his life in the soul by them. They are, if you like, exit points rather than entry points as far as showing a true spiritual experience is concerned. Many 'Christians' have never met God in their souls because they are still at the level of believing the right things, doing the right things and feeling the right things and calling them conversion. Many genuine Christians have falsely claimed the empowering of the Spirit because they identify him with their emotional feelings in a meeting or, worse, with a manipulated manifestation of 'spiritual' gifts. The true experience of God comes about by the Word of God experienced in the power of the Spirit.

The charismatic movement has done a great service to evangelical Christianity by placing back on our agenda the need for the Holy Spirit. But it has also done a great disservice by its concentration on emotion. It has allowed people to believe that the experiential part of Christian living is essentially focused inwards on either the Christian life or the worship of the church. The New Testament tells a different story. When the Spirit came people witnessed to their faith with spiritual authority. They still preached a doctrinally demanding and Bible-centred faith. They still spoke of Christ as the object of faith and means of knowing God. But they did so with divine authority which led people to repentance and faith.

The difference between pre- and post-Pentecost evangelism was not in the message but in the power of that message to convert the world. That is what is missing in modern evangelicalism whether of the conservative or charismatic kind. Both streams have large churches which are very successful in evangelism and discipleship. Both streams have struggling causes where numbers do not grow and the impact on society is minimal. It is too simplistic to think that charismatics have the Spirit while conservatives do not. What passes for authority in both circles may be nothing more than good packaging and confident church life. Confident in itself. The authority we need is God: God the Holy Spirit, speaking through God's own Word of truth. The postmodern world will be turned upside down by that, as the Roman world was two thousand years ago.

The Gift of the Holy Spirit

How should we restore the right experience of the Holy Spirit?

First of all, we must restore his place of honour in mission. The early Church was told in no uncertain terms that they could not go into the world without the power of the Spirit. In Acts chapter 1 we find a waiting church. In Acts chapter 2 we see an authoritative one. Many evangelical churches are still in Acts chapter 1. It may be argued that Pentecost is a once and for all time event which cannot be repeated and there are certainly elements in the story which suggest that – the shaken building, the rushing wind, the visible flames of fire. The Spirit was indeed given once and for all time to the Christian Church in the sense that God has never withdrawn his gift. Yet what is true in God's missionary purpose may not yet be true in the experience of the individual Christian or church. Two elements need to be added to the picture. The first is missionary commitment in evangelism and the second is our personal acknowledgement of need to fulfil that task. Like the first Christians we may be locked inside our own 'upper room', unwilling or unready to face the primary calling of the Christian life.

The challenge of Pentecost is not first of all one of empowering but one of empowering to preach the gospel. Many Christians are interested in power if it is to receive gifts and establish themselves in church life through spiritual gifts. Far fewer of us want to offer our lives to God in a momentous commitment to serve his kingdom purposes by witnessing to a lost world of Jesus Christ and his message of salvation. Pentecost is not about personal fulfilment or holiness but about boldness and authority to speak of Jesus Christ in the world. For that reason many Christians are deluded in their claims to baptism in the Spirit. They claim an experience, but what experience? The Holy Spirit has been reduced to performing tricks to keep the church together instead of empowering the church to send it into the world.

The second need of the evangelical church with regard to the Holy Spirit is to restore the place of believing and expectant prayer. We all know the dismal facts of 'the prayer meeting'. It is honoured by neglect, it is cold and formal, it is passionless even when it is held. The answer to this tragedy is faith. Unbelieving prayer is no prayer at all. There is no point in praying for conversions if we do not believe that God will answer, or if we believe that the reason for prayer is merely to be obedient or to keep the church a little more spiritual than otherwise it would be. The prayers which bring about Pentecost are fed by faith that God will hear and answer from heaven because his sovereign purpose is to save new generations of people for his glory. To ask God to save and then not to expect him to do so, is not to ask at all. What child comes to a father or mother to ask for something already convinced that the request will probably be refused?

Think of Christmas. You promise your children presents and ask what they would like. They may ask for things you are unwilling to give for their own best interests, but you have committed yourself to the fact of giving. God has committed himself to the fact of giving when we pray in faith to him. Not only that, he has told us what he will give us when we pray for people to be saved. Like children at Christmas we should be hanging up our stockings after a prayer meeting!

Spurgeon, the great nineteenth-century preacher told a story about this kind of faith. A young preacher came to him lamenting the lack of success in his ministry. He recognized that every week Spurgeon preached people were converted. Spurgeon replied, 'You don't expect converts every week do you?' and the man said, 'Of course not'. Spurgeon turned on him and said, 'That is why you don't get them!'

Who are the people who have most right to this authority? All those who are committed to sharing the good news of Christ and who believe that God has not changed his mind about winning and discipling the peoples of this world. Ministers and teachers, Sunday school workers and house group leaders, people who privately speak of their faith – whoever we are, we are called to speak of Christ and expect conversions as a result because we are as right as the gospel and as powerful as the Holy Spirit who enables us!

The gospel is a glorious message. The Spirit's ministry is a glorious ministry. The modern evangelical church is an inglorious institution more concerned with its inner workings and gifts than with winning the world of the next generation. Some want to be correct and orthodox. Others want to be emotionally moved and entertained. The true need is to see Pentecostal power for world mission repeated in the church today as we seek God for his anointing. The baubles of Christmas are not the substance of it. We evangelicals must take our eyes off how well our church is decorated by the Spirit's gifts and focus on the Christmas gift itself – a Saviour for the world. Even the postmodern world.

Twelve

A Church in Touch with the World

I have told you about my conversion. Now I want to tell you about the church in which I was converted. It was founded after the Welsh revival of 1904 to cope with the converts in a more congenial atmosphere than the mainstream church from which it split. Unfortunately, the church stood still in terms of its cultural expression. In the sixties when I first encountered it, the people were still singing the songs of 1900 – a Christian version of the music hall songs replete with choruses to each verse and sentimental stories in the lyrics. The worst song in the book was entitled *Where is my wandering boy tonight?* It was a particular favourite of a man who only had two daughters! The singing was awful. One lady had such a large vibrato in her voice that she managed to sing hymns in three keys at once! The church was in a time capsule totally out of touch with the 'swinging sixties' and I rather think it was proud of it.

I could not relate to that church! The only reason I went to it was the youth work was run by some teachers who held the meetings in their homes and presented the Christian faith in a way I could more easily relate to. My world was the one where the Campaign for Nuclear Disarmament preoccupied serious young people and the Beatles were just beginning to make their mark. I found I had to live in two worlds. The church was so different that I realized there was a gulf between my evangelical faith and life in the wider world.

Thirty years on the evangelical church has dramatically changed. It is much more aware of the world at large. Young people can go to churches where the same musical styles are used as in society at large, where the Bible version is modern and where you don't have to enter a time warp to be a Christian.

Yet I am not sure that we evangelicals are relating well to our society. Two things have been lost. One is our sense of identity apart from the unbelieving world. The other is an awareness that the world is a place which needs redemption rather than acceptance by us.

In the World but not of it

There is a biblical line to be drawn between the world of people God loves and 'this world' which stands under the judgement of God. 'This world' is the moral and spiritual climate of society, the underlying values it believes in and follows. The Christian is called to live in *the* world but not according to *this* world. That is the distinction we are losing in our generation. Consequently, people more and more tend to associate being 'in the world' with being like the world in matters of value, culture, entertainment and leisure. It makes for cheap grace. We can have Christ and have the world at the same time. When we do that we fail to understand why John commands the Christian

> *Do not love the world or anything in the world. If anyone loves the world, the love of the Father is not in him. For everything in the world – the cravings of sinful man, the lust of his eyes and the boasting of what he has and does – comes not from the Father but from the world. The world and its desires pass away, but the man who does the will of God lives for ever. (I Jn 2:15–17)*

The answer to living in 'this world' is to live according to God's kingdom values while we are here on earth. It is a question of motivation before it is one of choice. In the evangelical church of my youth the difference was shown by avoiding the fashions of our generation, both in clothes and music. We were also discouraged from watching television, reading novels or even voting, because those things were 'worldly'. To avoid being worldly we withdrew from the world into the programme of the church and ignored the world as a whole.

That was wrong. It suggested that culture was outside the pale of God's interest. Those of us who became Christians either became oddities to our friends or to the church. I was burdened from the first to win people like myself to the Christian faith. I knew the problems of living with unbelief and I wanted to remain close enough to my non-Christian friends to be able to communicate with them. It is unquestionably right that evangelicals have become much more committed to that ideal than thirty years ago.

On the other hand, the problem is at the other end of the scale today. Christians are so much a part of our culture that we either keep quiet about our faith or else do not try to relate it to any of our actions. The result is that Christians have little or no cutting edge and no critique of the world to offer.

At the Cutting Edge

This question of culture needs to be addressed again by evangelicals. The old mistake was to write it all off. The new mistake is to adopt it uncritically. The biblical way is to assert the lordship of Christ over everything. Christ is Lord. That is the great fact of the cross, the resurrection and the ascension into heaven. If he is Lord, then his lordship applies to everything we do, everything we think, everything we like.

Christ is the Lord of politics, the King of Kings and Lord of Lords. Therefore, politics must come under his control through agendas which establish his righteousness in public life and through the conduct of political life on biblical principles of truth and integrity and compassion. There is a need for Christian politicians and civil servants and police officers, whose aim is not simply to serve there as 'salt' against corruption but as 'light' to transform the world according to biblical truth. A great example of that ideal is Sir Fred Catherwood in our own generation.

Christ is the Lord of work. We should not approach our jobs as if we had only non-Christian standards to fulfil or the wishes of our employers to comply with. We are called to work hard, to produce good work to the glory of God and to choose spheres of work which do not conflict with the standards of God's kingdom. But being a Christian at work may also interfere with promotion or status. It may mean reserving time for family and church life although our employers expect us to live for them. It may mean formulating Christian policies of work and seeking to get them established in the market-place in the name of Christ. We need Christian experts in every field who are unashamed of the Christian faith and message. Christians often think that their Christian duty at work is fulfilled by evangelizing colleagues. That is not a work calling, but a kingdom one for the whole of our lives. The calling of work is fulfilled by applying biblical truth and biblical standards to the world of work.

Christ is Lord of art. There are some forms of film, music, literature and art which deny the truth, exploit sexuality, deny order in the universe and so on. The Christian is called to stand against all that is wrong and to uphold all that is right. We desperately need people to enter these areas of life in the name of Jesus Christ and assert his lordship. We are a long way from having so many Christians working in this area that they engage with each other as well as with their art so that distinctively Christian values emerge as art forms and styles.

One could continue to list every area of life from theatre to home-making. The lordship of Christ does not call us out of culture but into it in his name. The evils which fill our society are worse because Christians have forgotten their calling to be salt and light in accordance with Jesus' command. This world does not belong to Satan but to Christ. Satan is a usurper who parades his power and influence in the hope that Christians will leave him to his own devices. We have forgotten the command to '*resist the devil, and he will flee from you*' (Jas. 4:7). Evangelicalism has become so banal and populist that the serious thought that is needed for these endeavours is neglected and well nigh impossible. The third millennium dawns on us in a great spiritual vacuum which will be filled. If we do not fill it, some other religious movement will. Beware, evangelical church!

There are some good signs in the current evangelical scene in the much greater concern of evangelicals for social justice. But we must be careful of our motives here. There is a tendency for Christians to think that doing good things can replace proclaiming good news. The purpose of changing the world is not to win more people to Christ or to replace winning them to him with impressing them with us. The purpose of changing the world is to assert the lordship of Christ over the world. That still leaves people in need of personal faith in him as Saviour and Lord. Even if everyone became Christian we would still need to face the challenge of poverty and injustice. Even if no one becomes a Christian we must still assert the justice of God over society. We confuse evangelism and social justice when we make choices between them.

A Total Biblical Vision

What we need to relate evangelicalism to the world is an army of people whose lives are shaped by kingdom values and informed by biblical principles. What we need to win the world is another army of evangelical people who will give their lives away to Jesus Christ in mission. One symptom of our sickness here is the lack of people who will give themselves for a lifetime of service to God. Missionary agencies all make the same complaint. When they ask for helpers they get offers of one or two years' service before young people 'return to normal living'. A similar trend is current in Christian ministry. The average applicant now comes after a first career from which they have taken early redundancy or retirement. Those who offer for ministry straight from university are a mere handful by comparison. As a result, the ministry lacks people trained by a lifetime studying to understand the Bible and the calling of service.

The way into the next millennium is to develop a much more biblical faith within evangelicalism. We stand at a turning point in the history of the Western world. We have had three hundred years of 'modern society' and it is coming to an end. The post-modern movement is actually a revolution as great as the revolutions that established Communism or Fascism. The evangelical movement is essentially a product of the dying world of 'modernity', with its focus on individualism, intellect, reason and science. A new kind of evangelical faith is needed for the next generation or we will die out like the dinosaur, unable to adapt in the new climate of the postmodern world.

The problem is that postmodernism itself is not a coherent thing. It is more a protest against what has gone before. Like Cromwell's armies it is better at smashing the images and idols of the past than at creating a new order. For that reason, evangelicals need not be afraid to challenge the revolutionaries and look beyond the phase in which we now live. It is far more important that we re-establish our core values and concerns than that we make them in the image of the postmodern generation. That is the weakness of some of the so-called 'postevangelical' churches and writers. They are seeking to accommodate the evangelical faith to postmodern ideas by moving away from biblical truth. The real need is to go further back and consider what we can learn from previous biblical movements to evanglicalism, such as the Reformers and Puritans.

Their lesson, which is what this book seeks to spell out, is that there is no need for biblical Christianity to perish with the death of modernity. The third millennium needs a total biblical vision of the kind they espoused as a revolutionary new movement by which to shape their society. We need such an evangelicalism for tomorrow.

At the heart of that vision is what we make of the world. Evangelicals have lived in a comfortable relationship with modern society where they were able to borrow some major themes which made the gospel relevant. The prime example of this is the emphasis on personal conversion with less concern for churchmanship than the Puritans and Reformers had. They were able to do this because the church was strong in influence and importance in the modern world. Things have changed. In the postmodern age the church is now a huge irrelevance and so the relation between the church and the world must come to the top of our agenda. It can be summed up in three statements.

First, the church must become an alternative society which relates to but challenges the world. Second, the Christian faith must seek to redeem society by its claims to truth and justice. The postmodern world is in danger of rejecting truth altogether. The Christian Church must become a rock to the world, a witness to the truth which claims every sphere of human existence in the name of Jesus Christ. Third, Christianity must become a movement based on sacrifice and service to Jesus Christ and no longer be satisfied with self-service and self-improvement. We need to recover the missionary zeal which will not be satisfied until we have penetrated every part of the world with biblical faith and every sphere of society with biblical truth.

Thirteen

The Church as a Community of Faith

Postmodern society is a strange contradiction. On one hand people are totally preoccupied with themselves. On the other hand people act more in groups than a generation ago, whether at work as teams or in the youth culture as tribes. This is because we live at a turning-point between the modern and the postmodern world. The modern world, which began with the Enlightenment, has taught us to value individualism to the point now that we cannot see beyond ourselves in regard to the purpose of life. On the other hand, life is very lonely on your own and we need some sense of belonging in order to fill the void. The old place of community within the family has been lost and nothing yet is taking its place except more temporary and casual groupings which do not tend to last or produce stable relationships. In this situation the church dimension of evangelical life will become as crucial to explaining Christian faith as the stress on individual conversion was to previous generations.

The traditional evangelical message has been that you need Christ and therefore must turn to him. If you turn to Christ you will need fellowship with other Christians, otherwise your faith will grow cold. Do you notice the agenda in this message? The purpose of the church is to strengthen the individual in faith. The focus is still on the element of personal fulfilment as a Christian.

A Community to Belong to

Compare that with the New Testament. One of the uncomfortable facts for evangelicals is the place of baptism in the preaching of conversion. People did not become Christians on a purely personal level but through being baptized into the Christian Church. Acts 2:38–41 makes it very clear:

> *Repent and be baptized, every one of you, in the name of Jesus Christ for the forgiveness of your sins. And you will receive the gift of the Holy Spirit. The promise is for you and your children and for all who are far off for all whom the Lord our God will call.' With many other words he warned them; and he pleaded with them, 'Save yourselves from this corrupt generation.' Those who accepted his message were baptized, and about three thousand were added to their number that day.*

There can be no doubt that the moment of conversion was the occasion of baptism into the church. Evangelicalism glossed over this biblical emphasis for two reasons. Firstly, there were many people already baptized and attending churches who were nevertheless unconverted. Secondly, there was in existence (and still is) a long history of confusion over baptism and salvation. The popular belief was that salvation was automatic upon baptism and so evangelicals wanted to stress the difference between being baptized and being saved by faith in Christ. They wanted people to stop looking to their infant baptism as the source of salvation and instead turn personally to Christ.

The real point of associating baptism with conversion in the New Testament is that conversion absolutely involves entering the life of the Christian community. A Christian in biblical terms is not simply someone who has decided for Christ in his private thoughts but one who has decided for Christian community as well. There was no such thing as an unbaptized Christian or a Christian who did not belong to the community of the Christian Church.

This fact made the church central to the life of the Christian as the fundamental act of allegiance to Jesus Christ. That message was neglected by the evangelical emphasis on personal and private faith in Christ. It is now time for the evangelical church to become biblical in its doctrine of salvation! To become a Christian means to join the Christian community. Of course, neither joining the church nor being baptized in themselves make someone a born-again Christian. It is rather that baptism into the church and conversion belong together.

The difference can be understood better if we look at the relation of conversion to the new birth. The new birth, or regeneration, is the act of God. It is a miracle by which God implants spiritual life into someone who previously did not have it. So Jesus insists (Jn. 3:3–6):

> *'I tell you the truth, no one can see the kingdom of God unless he is born again.'*
>
> *'How can a man be born when he is old?' Nicodemus asked. 'Surely he cannot enter a second time into his mother's womb to be born!'*
>
> *Jesus answered, 'I tell you the truth, no one can enter the kingdom of God unless he is born of water and the Spirit. Flesh gives birth to flesh, but the Spirit gives birth to spirit.'*

It is the work of the Holy Spirit to create in us spiritual life. Peter makes the same point in 1 Peter 1:23: *'For you have been born again, not of perishable seed, but of imperishable, through the living and enduring word of God.'*

The Spirit gives life to the spirit of a man or woman. That is the new birth. Where, then, does conversion come into the equation? It is our human response to this new life. It is to turn from a life without God (repentance) and to trust in Christ as Saviour and Lord (faith). Conversion is the human moment of turning in response to the gospel. What we have done is to make that a purely private issue. Often, booklets on conversion advise people to find a quiet place on their own even, where they can pray and ask Jesus into their lives. Thereafter, they are to count themselves as true believers.

The New Testament Christians would have thought we were wrong! They said rather that if you want to turn from your old life of sin to trust in Christ as Saviour you must do it publicly by being baptized into the Christian community of faith. Hence Peter calls people to repent and be baptized for the forgiveness of sins. It is not that baptism has a magic power to give the Holy Spirit. It is not that the gift of the Spirit follows conversion. It is rather that the act of conversion in which we receive Christ is only completed by receiving his people on earth as the body of Christ in which we now have to live. Conversion was shared with the church as a public event.

This emphasis places a very different perspective on being a Christian. It means that the Christian faith is not only a personal choice but also a shared way of life. That is not an option to help the Christian but something entirely central to being a Christian. If the evangelical movement may be criticized over its doctrine of conversion it is in this. It has separated life for Christ from life with Christ in his body. In the postmodern age few people go to church out of tradition and the number of people who are automatically baptized, even in infancy, is falling. This new cultural situation provides the church with an opportunity to re-establish the biblical connection between conversion and baptism into the Christian Church.

The fact of the church is key to addressing postmodern society. The great vacuum in postmodern life is the lack of meaningful personal relationships. Marriage and family as stable units have gone. Divorces and broken homes cannot be undone. But there is a place where relationships can be profound, love real and human companionship lasting. It is the Christian family.

That is an enormous challenge to current church practice. Our churches have been moulded into the image of modern society. We attend when we feel like it, we reserve our commitment to its activities, we remain shallow with each other when we meet together. The modern church is too often a contradiction of the New Testament in its lack of spiritual reality and fellowship. It is possible to be a stranger to fellow Christians even after years spent in the same church together. How are we to change this situation?

Firstly, the message of the gospel must be focused more on baptism with conversion so that they are brought back together.

We must not count people as Christians until they fulfil the biblical mandate to turn from a godless world and enter the community of faith. The 'lone ranger' Christian must be unsaddled and his horse put out to graze!

There is no Christianity except church Christianity. Evangelicals have mocked 'churchianity' but we must learn to eat our words. Christianity is indeed churchianity in a very real sense, provided baptism is accompanied with faith. People are not truly converted unless they submit their lives to the authority of Jesus Christ and that is revealed primarily through submission to baptism into the church.

The question arises whether baptism before conversion is valid. One of the reasons evangelicals have maintained the separation of baptism from conversion is that so many people have been baptized in infancy and Scripture speaks of 'one baptism' (Eph. 4:5). This is not only an infant baptist problem, however. In churches which practise believers' baptism it is sometimes the case that young people are baptized during their teenage years on an inadequate basis. I have frequently found people saying to me that their 'believers' baptism' was based on peer pressure or an emotional decision which they thought was conversion but they have since realized was not. Should they then be re-baptized when they really come to Christ? My answer is yes. My reason is that baptism is not biblically valid unless it is accompanied by true repentance from sin and a genuine faith in Christ. It is an outward act which symbolizes an inward and spiritual experience of God's grace. If the inward experience is missing the outward act is meaningless. The Christian Church is not a community created by baptism but a community created by grace. Any tendency to remove the centrality of God's grace from its place in church life weakens the church and makes it less a society of redeemed people and more a compromised institution. The church of God will never be completely pure in morality because we remain sinners in practice even after conversion. But it should be as pure as possible in the sense that every member is born again of God's Spirit. When someone is shown not to be spiritually reborn, even after baptism, that person is not truly a member of God's people and the baptism they have undergone is an empty ceremony. I have to admit here that this is a controversial view, especially for those who are not 'believer baptists'. It is nevertheless the position I personally find in the New Testament.

Community in Practice

Secondly, church discipline must be restored to its biblical place. If the church is central to Christian living, the relation of the individual Christian to the church must be one of willing submission to its fellowship and teaching. We have become accustomed to individualism ruling church life to far too great an extent. If someone disagrees with their church's teaching that is deemed to be their choice. If someone chooses to live a life which denies the standards of Christianity we have become tolerant of the contradiction. Most especially, if someone speaks against fellow members or causes a divisive spirit in the church we have tended to treat that as a pastoral problem for the leaders to solve without bringing matters to the church for the preservation of church unity.

These three things are regarded in the New Testament as requiring expulsion from the church in the last resort. Doctrinal disagreement is dealt with in Galatians 1, and 2 John 10; immorality in 1 Corinthians 5; and division in Matthew 18:15–18. These activities have become tolerable in the modern church because we do not prize the unity of the church as the gift of God. We have turned it into a human institution where we feel free to make the rules without regard to God's standards. I am not advocating a loveless church here, but a church so characterized by love for Christ that we obey him.

Thirdly, mission must become the substantial purpose of the Christian Church after worship. Indeed, worship and evangelism are very closely related since 'worship' means to declare God's 'worthship'. Many evangelicals tell it to each other and then regard the task as complete. The fact is that the world must hear the good news of Jesus Christ.

The task of mission is not presently very credible to the world because the only time they hear from the evangelical church is when we want them to be converted. Credibility for the gospel depends on the whole biblical faith being proclaimed in the world, including the lordship of Christ is every sphere of existence. Our lack of penetration into politics and public life demeans our evangelism because the gospel is not seen in all its glory and fullness. That was the secret of the Puritan era. When the gospel addressed the status of King Charles and his government people may not have agreed with the political action of every Bible Christian (who disagreed among themselves anyway) but they did realize that their gospel addressed the whole of life.

Fourthly, the evangelical church needs to weigh carefully its cultural style. We need to express not only our empathy with the culture in which we live but also our distinctiveness from it. Too much worship today is at the level of entertainment rather than declaration, of comfort rather than challenge. There is a real need to find a balance between cultural empathy and cultural distinctiveness and both qualities need to be embodied in our worship. To some extent the Christian church needs to stand above the changes in culture around us or we will be sucked into the world as a church.

Fifthly, we need to understand the vital need for closeness and acceptance. There is no place called 'home' in the postmodern world. Families are broken apart by divorce, work moves them round the country and friendships are increasingly superficial. Love is largely absent from people's lives in terms of something which is secure and fulfilling. The promises of love are exaggerated while the disciplines of love are feared and ignored. The community of Christian believers is the answer to this huge vacuum in postmodern society. It must become a place where we mean it when we call each other 'brother' or 'sister', where the promises of love are kept and the disciplines of love made real.

Sixthly, we must get away from substituting evangelical 'rules' for biblical principles in church life. A good evangelical is too often identified with someone who behaves suspiciously like a middle class person in matters of dress and cultural taste. Education and sanctification have become confused, leaving less cultured people disfranchised as a result. Furthermore, evangelicals have an old definition of 'worldliness' which still marks out good from bad Christians. Old battles about alcohol and make-up and watching films survive from earlier generations in a way which is tedious if not offensive to many committed Christians, who find the evangelical world a suffocating one in its small-mindedness.

Worldliness in the Bible is more about living for money, pride and power than about personal fitness and physical discipline. Worldliness is more about the motives which drive us than about the habits we adopt. It is possible for someone to be self-disciplined over health and to be obsessed by worldly ambition. The evangelical church needs to concentrate on the big church issues again. Involvement in the life of the kingdom is what makes an unworldly Christian. He or she will be someone who does not live for the gains of this life but for the gains of the kingdom of God.

Finally, the evangelical church must beware the current preoccupation with structural church unity. It is right that we should seek to witness to the world of Christ through unity in the church. But the unity which convinces the world of the truth is not a structural one but a spiritual one based on confessing Christ as Saviour and Lord according to the Scriptures. Our evangelistic vision may become deflected into schemes for organizational union. This must be clear to us. The gospel saves, not the church. The passion we need in order to confront the world of the next millennium is a passion to win people to Jesus Christ and the truth about him revealed in Scripture. Unless we are people of the truth we are no witnesses at all.

The biblical faith has been undermined more by the contradictions, lack of biblical clarity and worldliness of the church than by its method of government. The great need of our generation is not to restructure the church according to the latest management techniques or the best inter-church strategies, but to reform her according to the teachings of Jesus Christ and his apostles. The church which brings itself under that teaching is equipped to face the world of the next millennium. The church which ignores that challenge will have nothing to say, however well structured it may be or however co-operative with other churches.

The great need of the modern church is to know the Bible and preach it and to know the Spirit's empowering and live in it. Such a church will succeed in the postmodern age. It will be a bastion against unbelief and sin, a fortress in which the believer will be safe, a rescue mission in which the lost world may find the reality and truth about God. May we be such a church!